Gender Images
in Public
Administration

To the women of public administration
—especially the students

Gender Images in Public Administration

Legitimacy and the Administrative State

Camilla Stivers

SAGE Publications
International Educational and Professional Publisher
Newbury Park   London   New Delhi

For information address:

 SAGE Publications, Inc.
2455 Teller Road
Newbury Park, California 91320

SAGE Publications Ltd.
6 Bonhill Street
London EC2A 4PU
United Kingdom

SAGE Publications India Pvt. Ltd.
M-32 Market
Greater Kailash I
New Delhi 110 048 India

Printed in the United States of America

Library of Congress Cataloging-in-Publication Data

Stivers, Camilla.
   Gender images in public administration: legitimacy and the administrative state / Camilla Stivers.
        p. cm.
   Includes bibliographical references and index.
   ISBN 0-8039-4802-6 (cloth) 0-8039-4803-4 (paper)
   1. Women in public life—United States. 2. Women in the civil service—United States. 3. Sex role—United States. 4. Public administration—United States. I. Title.
HQ1391.U5S75   1993
305.42'0973—dc20   92-32145
                                                                     CIP

93 94 95 96 10 9 8 7 6 5 4 3 2

Sage Production Editor: Astrid Virding

Contents

Preface

The roots of this book go back to the early 1980s, when I was an administrator in the nonprofit sector and a middle-aged doctoral student. At the time, my feelings about feminism were like those of many women today—ambivalent. In the 1960s, the so-called second wave of feminism had been a source of empowerment, helping me to move beyond a good bit of self-blame and, I believe, nudging open a few occupational doors. I had briefly subscribed to *Ms.* magazine and even attended one meeting of the local chapter of the National Women's Political Caucus. But my energies were absorbed by my career and raising my two sons, and besides, I wasn't sure that I really wanted to be "militant." I told myself I wanted to get ahead on the basis of my talents, not because I was a woman.

In 1981, I enrolled at Virginia Tech's Center for Public Administration and Policy. Launched on my doctoral studies, I occasionally grumbled to myself about the absence of discussion about women's issues, the all-male faculty, the fact that we never seemed to read anything written by a woman (except for good old Mary Parker Follett), the articles that used *he* and *his* for the whole human race. I kept these complaints to myself, however; I wanted to be seen as a good student. I guess I hoped that my professors wouldn't notice—or at least attach any significance to the fact— that I was a woman. They were supportive of my efforts, and I was (and still am) grateful for that and for what they taught me.

Then came lengthy conversations with fellow student Jackie Cook, with her gentle but persistent appeals to my conscience. As the result of many talk sessions with Jackie and other women students, I began to see both the absence of women from the course material and my own distance from women's concerns as moral issues. My intellectual curiosity was also aroused; I began to do some reading in feminist theory and decided that I would do a paper on "something to do with women and public administration"—something that would explore the ways in which a feminist perspective might change thinking in the field. To prepare myself, I went back through *Public Administration Review,* intending to build on what had already been written. I was shocked (a sign of my naïveté) to find that in the past decade there had been almost nothing written from a feminist viewpoint: only a symposium edited by Nesta Gallas (1976) and one or two other articles with an equal opportunity focus. Only Bob Denhardt and Jan Perkins's article (1976) broached the question of a paradigm shift. It seemed impossible (at the time), but despite what I knew was an outpouring of feminist work in political theory, organizational sociology, and even economics, public administration theory appeared to be innocent of a feminist theoretical perspective. That discovery changed my view of the field and what I might have to contribute to it. I've been playing out the implications ever since.

As the book notes, feminism is under something of a cloud currently, so it seems important for me to say both of two things: First, I believe women and men in public administration need not call themselves feminists to take seriously the question of the impact of gender on our concepts and normative theories; second, I hope that despite the occasional appearance of the term *feminist* in what follows women and men will see my argument as an invitation to dialogue regardless of their individual comfort level with the label. I am now glad to apply the term to myself, but I don't insist that anyone else do so in order for us to have a conversation.

It is customary at this point in such exercises to acknowledge the help of others, but my impression is that no woman gets to the point of finishing a book without an awareness of debts whose depth goes way beyond the dimensions of ritualistic thanks. I have the sense of being in a network of mutual aid, one at whose center I seemed to be for a brief moment. It would have been literally impossible for me to do this book without that network, and I hope in the future to be able to support and nourish others as I have been supported and nourished.

Guy Adams read the manuscript in draft with a level of care, discernment, and promptness that are an author's most fervent wish. Kathy Denhardt, Cynthia McSwain, Orion White, Lucia Harrison, Dean Olson, Cheryl King, Zahid Shariff, and the Evergreen students in the fall 1991 version of Political and Economic Context of Public Administration also read the entire draft with unsparing critical faculties and a wealth of good ideas. The comments of several anonymous reviewers also saved me from some of my more egregious intellectual follies. John Marvin continued to put up with me when nobody should have been expected to; Jackie Cook, as I indicated above, put me on the path. Ruth-Ellen Joeres gave me a crucial month's haven complete with a "desk of my own," and a lifetime of friendship. Bonita Evans and Jane Lorenzo graciously provided professional assistance with the manuscript preparation. Many other friends and colleagues offered priceless encouragement and moral support. The Evergreen State College provided sponsored research funds during the summers of 1989 and 1991. Harry Briggs at Sage Publications has been unfailingly helpful and enthusiastic. Words can't do the thanking; I only hope some future actions of mine in support of others will begin to.

1

Gender Dilemmas and the Quest for Legitimacy in Public Administration

Defending the legitimacy of administration has been a continuing theme in American political thought since the founding period. The administrative state needs justification because the exercise of discretionary power by unelected career administrators strains principles of representative democracy. In theory, power flows from the people to their elected representatives and indirectly to executive and judicial officials. The power of those who govern is checked by the fact that citizens can vote them out of office or at least vote out those who appointed them. In such a system, the exercise of power by tenured civil servants, neither elected nor easily removable, is problematic. Yet career administrators commonly make decisions that amount to binding answers to questions that have public interest dimensions. Their interpretations of policy mandates put flesh on the bare bones of vague and often internally contradictory laws. Administrators exercise regulatory authority, judged on a case-by-case basis, over the activities of private corporations and individuals. Career officials in bureaucratic agencies decide whether certain individuals, organizations, or communities meet the guidelines that qualify them for the benefits of public programs. Administrators have power.

Perhaps the most famous argument in defense of public administration was Woodrow Wilson's (1887/1978) in an essay now widely accepted as the founding document in the field. Wilson argued in favor of a sharp separation between public administration and politics: The duty of administrators was simply to carry out legislative mandates by means of scientific expertise, not to take sides on political questions. Administration was legitimate because it was neutral. Over time, observers have come to regard this position as too simplistic and inconsistent with the realities of bureaucratic life. Conventional wisdom now recognizes the impossibility of segregating administration and politics. Yet professional expertise still serves as a major basis for the justification of public administration. The question remains, as Mosher's (1968) classic study puts it, "How can a [professional] public service . . . be made to operate in a manner compatible with democracy?" (p. 3). As the administrative state (government by administrators) has burgeoned and growing numbers of Americans have had direct experience with it, the question has become increasingly urgent.

Skepticism about bureaucrats is an ongoing American phenomenon; the late 20th century, however, constitutes something of a nadir in the fortunes of public administration. During the last two decades or so, civil servants have borne the brunt of widespread public suspicion and outright disapproval. Trading on the reported failure of the War on Poverty, swelling budget deficits, and a series of scandals that sharpened Americans' misgivings about government activism, politicians have promised to lower taxes, reduce the size of the bureaucracy, and clean up "waste, fraud, and abuse." Republicans and Democrats alike, including presidential candidates, have castigated public employees as paper shufflers and time servers, enmeshed in red tape and out of touch with reality. The public's estimation of bureaucrats, never high to start with, has sunk even lower in response. Not surprisingly, the need to defend the administrative state has seemed particularly acute in recent years.

The field of public administration has reacted to the onslaught of criticism with a concerted effort to justify the place that career administrators hold in the American system of government. Celebrations surrounding the constitutional bicentennial and the 100th anniversary of Wilson's founding essay unleashed a flow of books, articles, special journal issues, and conference presentations aimed at validating public administration. For example, Goodsell's (1985) *The Case for Bureaucracy* pointed to the effectiveness of bureaucratic activities, while Rohr's (1986) *To Run a Constitution* argued that the administrative state was consistent with constitutional principles. Many efforts to justify public administration draw attention to the public servant's essential qualities; these arguments invoke images of the expertise, leadership, or virtue of public administrators as individuals or as a group (Mitchell & Scott, 1987). The thrust of these defenses is that the scale and complexity of late-20th-century society demand the existence of a stable class of career officials who can be counted on to have the competence, the vision, and the public spirit to steer the ship of state.

During the same period that public administration has labored to defend itself, an equal or greater volume of writing has been calling into question the gender dimensions of Western political philosophy. This work, usually classified as women's studies or feminist theory, critiqued the liberal state for its marked individualism and for the dependence of its clear boundary between public and private spheres on the exclusion of women and women's concerns from political life. Feminist theory offered new theories of power, of virtue, of the nature of organization, and of leadership and professionalism and brought to light fundamental ways in which women have shaped society and politics. Yet few if any of these ideas have made their way into conversations in public administration, and defenses of the administrative state show no apparent consciousness that the legitimating images of public administration have gender dimensions or that the gender dynamics of Western politics might be significant to their project.

One could argue that apologists for the administrative state seem insensitive to gender because an enterprise so roundly castigated by politicians and the public at large hardly needs further criticism. What help to public administration could a feminist point of view possibly be? Probably little, it would appear, if (as many of the current defenses would suggest) justifying public administration involves simply mobilizing support for administrative business as usual. My underlying assumption, however, is that public administration's legitimacy problem has deeper roots than the failure of the War on Poverty, Watergate, Iran-Contra and other scandals, and Reaganism; therefore, the need for legitimacy cannot be handled by an argument that restricts itself to currently accepted considerations.

The thesis of this book is that the images of expertise, leadership, and virtue that mark defenses of administrative power contain dilemmas of gender. They not only have masculine features but help to keep in place or bestow political and economic privilege on the bearers of culturally masculine qualities at the expense of those who display culturally feminine ones. Far from being superficial window-dressing or a side effect, the characteristic masculinity of public administration is systemic: It contributes to and is sustained by power relations in society at large that distribute resources on the basis of gender (although not solely on this basis) and affect people's life chances and their sense of themselves and their place in the world.

Looking at public administration through the lens of gender, its public dimensions are revealed as gender dimensions. The fact that there is any need to defend public administration can be traced to the public nature of its authority. The decisions of public administrators bind others outside public agencies to do or refrain from doing certain things. Public administration involves the discretionary exercise of public power, and we expect public power to justify itself. Typically, this is accomplished by reference to redeeming features such as the public interest dimensions of administrative decision making, the expertise that is said to serve the public good, and the necessity for public-spirited administrative leadership in an era of postindustrial complexity. But this publicness is problematic, because it is grounded in an historical understanding of the public sphere as a male preserve, distinct from the domestic realm that has been the primary life space and responsibility of women.

Classical liberalism has always seen boundaries around the public sphere as necessary to prevent tyranny, by sheltering individual, "private" concerns from the reach of the state. But paradoxically, the viability of liberal society, hence its public sphere, depends on the fulfillment of certain functions in the household, such as the provision of shelter, food, and clothing and the bearing and nurturing of children. Both pervasively in theory and persistently in practice, the household has been viewed as the realm of women; and women's concerns, when they revolve around their domestic responsibilities, have been seen as private—not political—by definition. Therefore, not only the justice of household arrangements but also *the division of human concerns into public and private* in the first place are barred from public discussion. Throughout history, women have been expected to handle needs related to sustenance and nurturance in order that men could have the time and energy for public pursuits.[1] This division of labor persists today despite equal opportunity and affirmative action policies, which have simply enabled women to shoulder both private and public responsibilities rather than to share them equally with men, and despite recommendations for shared parenting, which are honored more in the breach than in the observance (see Hochschild, 1989; Rhode, 1988).

Like other public sector activities, public administration is structurally male despite its apparent neutrality: It can only go on as it does because women bear a lopsided share of the burden of domestic functions without which life would simply not be possible. Thus justifications of public administration take place in a space that (1) depends for its coherence on the subordination of women through their assignment to a set of duties that, no matter how necessary, are generally regarded as less worthy or significant and (2) limits both women's opportunities to participate in public life and the time and energy they have to devote to it.

The gender dimensions of this arrangement are paradoxical. The state depends on the household, but acknowledges only grudgingly the political relevance of domestic issues (consider how long it took for spouse and child abuse to become a policy concern); throughout liberal theory women are treated as "citizens" but in reality their participation in public life has been restricted, either formally (in law) or practically (by the demands of their household duties).

It is this sort of gender paradox, which I argue constitutes a dilemma for women in the administrative state, that the book considers. Examining gender dilemmas involves taking into account everyday life practices, such as what goes on in families, organizations, and politics, as well as what theorists say. It entails an effort to undo the taken-for-grantedness of administrative practices and what is written and thought about them: to bring to light ambiguities, gaps, contradictions, and unspoken assumptions that are connected to our notions of what constitutes appropriate masculine and feminine behavior—that is, gender. The intent is to articulate the harm these administrative ideas and patterns of behavior work on women and to lay the groundwork for the transformation of the thoughts and practices in question. I want to show that these widely accepted understandings devalue women's contributions and concerns, and limit their political and social freedom. Gender dynamics do, of course, restrict men's options as well, because the range of pursuits and behavioral styles they feel free to adopt are narrower than they would be if men did not have to worry about being thought "feminine." But in most cases, the coherence of the patterns of thought in question depends on maintaining women in a disadvantageous position relative to men; therefore, their impact on women is more severe.

Examining gender dilemmas in public administration does not imply the view that other factors such as race and class are less important. Gender-based oppression is tied to oppression that is race- or class-based; gender's importance is not as *the* source of domination but as a lens that enables one to see things that other lenses may miss. This awareness has finally dawned as the result of criticism by women of color and working-class and poor women, who pointed out the narrowness of what had passed for feminism. They noted, for example, how the work of white middle-class feminists established themselves as the standard of womanhood, replicating men's time-worn assumption that they were the human norm and women the exception. These protests open the prospect of a theory of women's experiences and place in society that results from interaction among the widest possible array of women (Lugones, 1991): one that treats various differences differently instead of attempting to reduce them prematurely—perhaps ever—to a common denominator. I try to maintain that prospect in mind as I proceed.

My approach to gender dilemmas in public administration is to focus on images of expertise, leadership, and virtue that have characterized defenses of administrative power. I do not pretend here to take on public administration as a whole (whatever the reader's own definition of that enterprise may be), although I think it needs taking on. In the main, the book is a consideration of what role certain ideas play in *one* aspect of *normative* public administration theory. Because of the connection I see between what we think and material realities in the world, however (as well as because I do not want readers to perceive the argument as excessively cerebral and inapplicable to their own experiences), I begin by considering through the lens of gender some things that are actually going on in the world of contemporary public administrative practice. Chapter 2 looks at the extent of women's historical progress as public employees, the peculiar nature of the organizational reality they experience, women's place in the political economy and the extent to which it is shaped by the administrative state. I examine the implications of these factors for our understanding of the nature of public organizational dynamics and of the special role in governance that public servants play. I suggest that facts such as that women are paid less than men, generally do most of the lower-level work, do not fit accepted managerial roles, experience sexual harassment in organizations, and work a double-shift of home and job responsibilities are as tangible as many other factors in the real world of public administration to which observers have given considerably more attention. I argue that our commonsense notions of the administrative state are deeply dependent on traditions that privilege men and the pursuits considered suitable for them over women and their work.

The book then turns to three images in defenses of public administration that I argue present women with dilemmas on the basis of gender. Chapter 3 deals with the image of expertise found in the argument that public administration is legitimate because public administrators are expert professionals. The need for expertise is a central tenet of modern public administration and has been so at least since Woodrow Wilson put forward the idea of a politics-administration dichotomy. I question four aspects of the reigning model of professional expertise: its aura of objectivity, its assertion of autonomy, its hierarchalism, and its norm of brotherhood. My argument is that, as it is currently constructed, the image of expertise is fundamentally inconsistent with widely accepted notions of womanhood and requires a social order that subordinates women.

Chapter 4 considers the leadership of the public administrator and the argument that, in a system of government marked by separation of powers and interest group politics, someone has to steer the ship of state, to be the balance wheel or fulcrum, to hold things together, to move them forward—to have a vision. I argue that this way of thinking about leadership works to keep in place dynamics of discrimination against women. Four images of public sector leadership are examined: the visionary, the decision maker, the symbol, and the definer of reality. As constituted, these ideals of leadership conflict with expectations about women's behavior, thus presenting them with a dilemma that requires them to manage the tension between being feminine and being a leader. I suggest that the current images of leadership are an undesirable basis on which to defend administrative power.

Chapter 5 examines arguments grounded in the public administrator's virtue, such as those that suggest that public administrators are legitimate because they are guardians or trustees of the public interest, or "citizens for the rest of us," or "heroes," or "exemplars of virtue." I suggest that images of virtue in American political history are fundamentally gendered and linked to a sex-based division of social life into public and domestic spheres that disadvantages women and hinders public administration from promoting a politically compelling version of virtue.

Obviously these three modes of argument—expertise, leadership, and virtue—are interrelated; I separate them mainly for the purposes of analysis. In chapter 6, I rejoin the three strands in an examination of the reform era out of which public administration as a self-conscious entity developed and in which so many of its ideas and arguments have their roots. The discussion aims to show how women's work and thought were at the center of the movement toward governmental reform: how themes of expertise, leadership, and virtue, blended in a rhetoric surrounding the tension between democracy and efficiency, public and private, were fundamentally shaped by the public spirited actions of women and by society's understanding of their social role. I argue that the extent to which the contemporary administrative state has roots in women's benevolent work has been obscured because male reformers, painted by party politicians as effeminate, felt the need to make public administration masculine by making it "muscular" and businesslike.

In the final chapter, I reflect on some of the implications of the book's arguments, that is, on what gender dilemmas inherent in current defenses of public administration tell us about the direction in which it must head if the administrative state is to be a

realm equally hospitable to women and men. This chapter presents some initial thoughts about what legitimate public administrative power might be. After offering a definition of feminism I suggest, in line with current feminist theories, that change must begin (as does this book) by focusing on aspects of current thinking that depend for their coherence on contrast—on delineating what it *is* at least partly by saying what it is *not*. The areas of vulnerability to change are those where gender has infiltrated thinking in public administration despite all efforts to maintain its neutrality, its apparent lack of gender. I play out a number of the possibilities for reshaping administrative theory and practice that appear as the result of gender analysis. The book concludes with a more in-depth feminist treatment of one normative theory of administrative discretion, the one that sees it as the exercise of practical wisdom (*phronesis*), as an example of the kind of alteration in our thinking that feminism could likely produce.

In a real sense, however, teasing new theory from the contrasts presented by masculinity and femininity will get us only part of the way. It will, I hope, stimulate people to reflect on a few of public administration's unexamined assumptions and to see the structural way in which the administrative state is dependent on women's double burden of household work and paid employment. As Ursula LeGuin (1974) has said, however, "Opposition maintains that which it challenges. . . . The point is to take a different road" (p. 153).

In this book I have chosen to focus the gender lens on defenses of the administrative state rather than elsewhere in public administration theory because it seems to me that expression of the most central values in the field become clearest where adherents seek to justify and defend the coherence and worth of their chosen object of study and practice. My aim is not to make a conclusive statement, even in the limited sector of thought with which this book deals, but to raise issues and stimulate discussion. Many of the topics I explore need and deserve treatment in greater depth, and some of the observations I make are speculative. In my view, where looking through the lens of gender will take public administration is still an open question, one that is best addressed in the most inclusive dialogue possible; I only insist that it is time to have this dialogue.

The implications of my argument for public administrative practice are twofold. First, the structural nature of public administration's masculinity means that equal opportunity and affirmative action strategies for advancing women's careers in public service, important though they are as a matter of sheer justice, cannot be counted on in and of themselves to change the tenor of public administrative affairs. As long as we go on viewing the enterprise of administration as genderless, women will continue to face their present Hobson's choice, which is either to adopt a masculine administrative identity or accept marginalization in the bureaucratic hierarchy. In either case, the intellectual assumptions, definitions of knowledge, and values that shape administrative thinking—and in turn the conditions of people's lives—are likely to remain as masculine, and as disadvantageous to women, as they now are.

A second implication of this exploration of public administration theory is that changes in thinking *can* effect changes in material circumstances: that developing an understanding of the connections between habits of thought and societal arrangements—between the ideas and values of public administration and systematic inequities in the conditions of people's lives—can lead human beings to take concrete actions that will change things for the better. Thus my position is that altering the composition of the public administration "choir" will do little unless its members become conscious of the need to sing different tunes from the ones currently in the repertoire, but that given the latter, much is possible.

NOTE

1. The literature is substantial. See, for example, Jaggar (1983), O'Brien (1989), and Okin (1989).

2

"On Tap but Not on Top":
Women in the Administrative State

Since Woodrow Wilson wrote the first scholarly paper on public administration, material realities have influenced images of administrative governance. Wilson's (1887/1978) statement that it was "getting harder to *run* a constitution than to frame one" (p. 4) was made in light of new economic and political complexities facing those charged with the execution of the public's business. Today's defenses of public administration continue to be attuned to the practical implications of such factors as a federal system of government, market economy, interest group politics, bureaucratic organizational form, the characteristics of fiscal and human resources, computerization, and other concrete aspects of the American administrative state in the late 20th century. To do otherwise would be to risk irrelevance, a charge that theorists in an applied field are more than usually anxious to avoid.

Yet public administration theory has been curiously insensitive to the gender dimensions of political, economic, and social factors

11

that affect public bureaucratic practices. Judging from the attention they devote to other structural and practical factors, it would seem that those who write about public administrators as experts, leaders, and heroes believe it important to take "the real world" into account in their reflections. Against this backdrop their failure to pay heed to gender appears to indicate that they see it as relatively insignificant in their field of observation. On the basis simply of reading arguments in defense of the administrative state, one might conclude either that there are no women in public administration or that, although they are there, the nature of their participation, their experience of public organizational life, their career opportunities and patterns, and their problems, are so little different from those of men as to have no effect—or at least none worth taking into account—on the substance of public administration from which these images are drawn.

The purpose of this chapter is to set the stage for a critique of this literature by suggesting that such is not the case. Women have been government employees now for more than a century and a quarter, and from the first days of their entry into public employment they had work experiences, career opportunities, and problems unique to them. I want to raise questions about the fact of women's presence in public bureaucracies instead of taking it for granted and to argue that their experiences are both different from men's and significant in their own right. In my view, our understanding of the real world of public administration—hence any theory about it—is incomplete without taking into account the terms of women's relationship to the administrative state. I will suggest that women in public administration are quintessentially "on tap" but still rarely "on top" and that this tangible circumstance is as important as any in painting a picture of public administration complete enough to serve as an adequate basis for theory. The discussion begins with a brief review of the history and current status of women in the career civil service; then I deal with organizational realities that women face (including those in public service), which I argue are materially different from men's; next is a consideration of the gender dimensions of the administrative state, that is, the mutual shaping that occurs between women's lives and the dynamics of *public* administration; finally, I reflect on the implications of these material realities for defenses of administrative governance. The discussion aims not to speak the definitive word on its subject but to raise issues and stimulate dialogue.

WOMEN IN PUBLIC SERVICE

Women first began to work in government in 1861, when the U.S. Department of the Treasury hired them to clip and count paper currency, replacing men who were needed as soldiers. Congress enacted legislation authorizing the hiring of women at $600 per year, or half the salary of the lowest-paid male clerk. Women thus enabled the federal government to meet a critical wartime need for more workers without straining its budget. Once inside the door, women stayed in the federal government; counting currency remained an exclusively female function for the rest of the century (Aron, 1987).

As Aron (1987) points out, the mixing of the sexes in offices was a bold experiment. Women had worked in factories since the 1820s, particularly in textile mills, where they were the majority of the work force by 1831 (Clinton, 1984). But the women hired to work for the Treasury Department were not working-class "girls" but "ladies," who in taking white-collar jobs as clerks violated the notion of separate spheres—men in the public sphere, women restricted to the private—that structured middle-class social life. "Government offices were clearly men's turf. One had only to look at the spittoons that adorned every office" (Aron, 1987, p. 163). Yet for many women the concept of separate spheres had always been more political ideology than economic reality. The *economic* public sphere, the world of factories, mills, and stores, had included both men and women virtually from the day "work" began to move outside the household. But the liberalist idea of a *political* public sphere distinct from the private, when linked to widespread ideas about women's proper role, barred women from full citizenship at the same time that a burgeoning capitalist economy made use of them. The notion of separate spheres, then, served to exclude women from political benefits but not to protect them from economic exigencies. Permitting women to take part in government, even at so lowly a level, was a significant breach in the gender-based wall between public and domestic rather than in any real barrier between government and business activity.

Women's entrance into public employment occurred on a different basis from the charity work that, although men shared it, had been uniquely feminine from its inception. Women invaded the male world of government employment "not because [it] required women's benign, compassionate, and caring influence, but because federal offices needed cheap labor and middle-class women needed good jobs" (Aron, 1987, p. 182). The need was such that by 1870 there were nearly 1,000 female federal employees, about 16% of the total in Washington, D.C.

Aron (1987) suggests that some of the problems that plague women workers today were evident even in the early decades of their involvement in public employment, including sexual harassment and discriminatory treatment. For example, in 1864 (only 3 years after women were first hired), a special congressional committee had to look into "certain charges against the Treasury Department" that seem to have entailed male supervisors attempting to win sexual favors from their female employees. In 1869, John Ellis's *The Sights and Sounds of the Nation's Capital* commented that "The acceptance of a Government clerkship by a woman is her first step in the road to ruin" (quoted in Aron, 1987, pp. 166-167). The first annual report of the Civil Service Commission observed that the new merit system would particularly benefit female job seekers because it would obviate the necessity for them to exert political influence or resort to "importunate solicitation, especially disagreeable to women" (Aron, 1987, p. 100). As early as the decade from 1884 to 1894, we find evidence of discrimination in hiring: During this period, women constituted between 28% and 43% of those passing civil service examinations, but only 7% to 25% of those actually hired—a disparity that reflects the exercise of discretion on the part of the appointing officer in the particular agency (Aron, 1987, pp. 109-110).

According to Harley (1990), black women were among those who applied for and received federal jobs during the 19th century; but black males held most of such higher level positions as were "reserved for blacks in Washington, D.C. throughout the 1880-1930 period" (p. 163). Brooks-Higginbotham (1989) argues that

> black women in the District [of Columbia] did not benefit from the feminization of clerical work in the late nineteenth century as did white women. . . . Racism confined the great majority to domestic service and thus presented them with fewer options than black men for upgrading their class position or working conditions. (pp. 131-132)

Then, as now, sex and race interacted to hinder women of color more than white women in their efforts to seek employment.

World War I marked a significant change in the public sector participation of women, not only furthering the cause of suffrage but bringing increasing numbers of women into both paid and volunteer work for the war effort. The Woman's Committee of the U.S. Council of National Defense coordinated a wide variety of activities on the part of women, stimulating housewives' food conservation, working with the Children's Bureau to save the lives of thousands of infants, and investigating conditions of women workers in war industries. "College girls worked on farms, women lawyers on exemption boards, women draftsmen [sic] in the Navy Department, and women physicians in hospitals in France" (Lemons, 1973/1990, pp. 16-17). Women demonstrated that they could do the work as well as the men they collaborated with or replaced, and new demands for equal opportunity and equal pay were heard.

The interest of feminists of the time in furthering the cause of equal opportunity employment led to the creation of the Women's Bureau in 1920, the first policy development entity in the federal government focused specifically on the needs of women:

> Women did not want an agency just to collect statistics about industrial women; they wanted a special counsel in government and continuous attention to the needs of wage-earning women. They wanted an open channel to present the problems of women, to give the woman's point of view. (Lemons, 1973/1990, p. 27)

While the creation of the bureau was cause for feminist celebration, their joy was tempered by provisions in the authorizing legislation that excluded bureau employees from a postwar bonus of $240 given to other federal workers and set the salaries of bureau statisticians at $1,800 to $2,000 per annum when statisticians in the Bureau of Labor Statistics were receiving $2,280 to $3,000 (Lemons, 1973/1990, p. 30). During the 1920s women were employed in government in increasing numbers, but virtually all of them were in clerical positions (Lemons, 1973/1990, p. 230). Harley (1990) notes that between 1920 and 1930 "racism in the federal government began to push black women and men out of white collar job opportunities. . . . Black federal employees who maintained their positions were increasingly victimized by racially-inspired policies and practices, such as segregated offices, cafeterias, and restrooms" (p. 164). This was a trend, public administrationists should note, set in motion under Woodrow Wilson's presidency and with his approval.[1]

The onset of the Depression extended overtly exclusionary practices to white women as well. Soaring unemployment rates made working women, especially those who were married, the target of efforts to restrict available jobs to men, on the theory that women worked for pin money. State and local governments passed laws barring women from public employment; they were joined by the federal government in 1932. Section 213 of the Economy Act required personnel cuts to be made by releasing "persons" whose "spouses" were also employed by the government (the original wording, deleted in committee, was *married woman* rather than *person*). Many women were forced to search desperately for alternative work, which almost always paid less; protests led to the bill's repeal in 1937 (Lemons, 1973/1990, pp. 230-231).

During World War II women flooded into a multitude of jobs from which they had previously been excluded, and despite the postwar emphasis on domesticity and "togetherness," women's labor force participation continued to rise as it had throughout the 20th century. Women constituted 26.5% of all employed workers in 1940, but their share had risen to 35% by 1960. During the same period, the percentage of female federal government workers lagged behind private sector levels, but did increase from 22.7% to 25% (U.S. Bureau of the Census, 1940, 1960).

A revived women's movement beginning in the mid-1960s set in motion a new expansion in the proportion of employed women, one that apparently has yet to crest. By 1970, just over 33% of full-time federal government workers were women, although as yet they were heavily concentrated in lower grade levels: only 3%

of workers in grades 13 to 15 were female and only about 1% in grades 16 to 18. By 1987, women constituted 48.2% of all federal employees: 14.2% in grades 13 to 15, and 6.9% in grades 16 to 18 (U.S. Bureau of the Census, 1990). A similar pattern can be observed in the case of state and local governments, for which women constituted 34.7% of full-time workers in 1973; 41.0%, in 1980; and 41.8%, in 1987. In 1987, women made up 29.1% of state and local government officials and administrators, 48.1% of professionals, and 39% of technicians (U.S. Bureau of the Census, 1990). The number of women appointed to cabinet-level posts in state government doubled between 1981 and 1987 (Hale & Kelly, 1989). A study released early in 1992 found that the number of women in senior posts in state and local governments (department heads, division chiefs, deputies and examiners) ranged from 13.9% in Hawaii to 38.5% in Louisiana ("Few Women," 1992, p. A8).

A Hudson Institute (1988) report identifies the continued rise in the proportion of women workers as one of three "important demographic issues facing Federal managers" between now and the year 2000 (p. 27). In assessing the significance of this continuing trend for personnel policies and practices, the report acknowledges the structural disparity between the life circumstances of men and women and the likely influence of this disparity on policy decision making:

> Because Federal women, like most women within society, will continue to have the lion's share of the household and family responsibilities in addition to their jobs, there is little doubt that such current issues as day-care, benefit reforms, more flexible hours of work, leave time, and other policies will continue to be a source of debate. As women rise within the Federal bureaucracy to policymaking positions they are likely, within the limits of the law, to reinterpret Federal policies regarding work and families and to promote more family-oriented policies. (Hudson Institute, 1988, pp. 26-27)

Interestingly, while the report notes that the federal government is a leader in providing day-care services at the work site, it argues that "child care benefits are of no value to the majority of Federal employees" and suggests a "cafeteria" approach that might require employees needing day care to trade off other benefits in return. One wonders if the institute would encourage local governments to require taxpaying families with children to trade off fire protection or garbage collection for public education.[2]

A 1976 *Public Administration Review* symposium on women in public administration reflected growing interest within the profession over the impact of the trend toward sexual integration of the public sector work force. The symposium editor, Nesta Gallas (1976)—first woman president of the American Society for Public Administration—noted three pervading themes: "discrimination against, underrepresentation of, and underutilization of women in public administration" (p. 347). Contributions to the symposium generally reflected an "equal opportunity" focus—seeking a piece of the existing pie rather than questioning its ingredients. One article does argue the need for structural changes in the idea of career, calling for such strategies as permanent part-time promotion tracks, career tracks for couples, and assessment of achievement that "takes into account success in broad life experience as well as 'service to the agency' as narrowly defined" (Stewart, 1976, p. 362). Only Denhardt and Perkins's (1976) essay, however, opens up the issue of gender's potential impact on the conceptual terms with which public administration interprets its world. They explore the effect that feminist thinking might have on the notion of task-oriented, rationalistic, efficient "administrative man," and wager that

> The key to the potential impact of feminist thinking on organizations of the future may finally come in the radical feminist rejection of the notion of superior domination—either by men or other elites—and their adoption of the concept of the authority of personal experience. . . . They are . . . unwilling to give up personal responsibility for their own actions by submitting to the authority of some accepted theory or structure. (p. 384)

Denhardt and Perkins see in "radical feminist thought" the possibility of revivifying the notion of personal responsibility on the part of individual members of public organizations but caution that greater numbers of women will not be enough to produce significant change, because women in traditional organizations will continue to be pressed to conform to the model of administrative man. Change, they say, will take positive efforts on the part of feminists, such as the formation of support systems and consciousness raising.

In general, however, in the field of public administration there has been little attention paid to women other than to reflect on their growing numbers in public agencies and on issues such as sexual harassment or discrimination in hiring and promotion. While the relative lack of women in positions of significant authority is an unsolved problem, the steady rise in the ratio of women to men in public agencies is undeniable and a cause for rejoicing. That the growth in women's participation in public employment over the last 125 years has been as large as it has, however, makes the fact that normative theorists of public administration have ignored it all the more puzzling and problematic.

WOMEN'S ORGANIZATIONAL REALITY

Theorists wishing to defend themselves against the charge of neglecting women's presence in public administration might offer the argument that organizations are organizations and women are simply some of the workers in them—that women's experiences in organizations as well as the general circumstances of their lives reflect no significant difference from men's. This would be a curious position to take in a culture that expends as much energy as ours does on seeing to it that gender differentiations are maintained (Epstein, 1988). Nevertheless, it would seem helpful to the general cause of promoting public administration theorists' attention to gender to reflect briefly on some of the dimensions of women's organizational and life circumstances as various observers have noted them. My assumption is that if nearly half the inhabitants of the realm of public administration are having experiences that are not taken into account by theories of the administrative state's legitimacy then it is time to reexamine the bases of these arguments.

Sheppard (1989) notes the practical difficulty in bringing to light the disparity between women's and men's organizational realities:

Under the tremendous pressures for acceptance and conformity necessary to success at work in our social world, which are heightened greatly for women in a male-dominated environment, the differences in the ways in which women and men may formulate their experiences are generally not readily apparent. While women continue to demonstrate their capacity for succeeding at "men's work" and often excelling at it, we are realizing that under the surface of achievement, women are experiencing a work reality that differs from that of men in many ways. (p. 141)

According to Sheppard, to consider organizational structures as objective and neutral when men's customary practices and values still so clearly pervade them is an ideological position.

Her research shows that both men and women associate issues of sex and gender in organizations with femaleness; maleness simply is not considered remarkable because it blends so easily with standard organizational processes. Sheppard (1989) notes that sometimes women do experience stereotypically male behavior as a problem, but for them to address it openly requires such a fundamental challenge to prevailing norms that women often instead redefine problematic situations either by choosing to ignore tensions and ambiguities or by focusing on their own identities—in other words, by seeing their own behavior or perceptions rather than men's as the source of the particular difficulty. For this reason, research that relies on self-reporting, particularly that in which women are found to perceive little dissonance between themselves and prevailing practices, must be interpreted with caution.

The problem for women members of organizations is how to manage their femaleness. Because expectations (widely shared by both women and men) about how managers and leaders will behave conform to expectations of male but not of female behavior, women must make deliberate efforts to balance conflicting roles. "Without constant vigilance regarding gender (and sexual) self-presentation, these women perceive that they run the risk of not being taken seriously, not being heard, and not receiving information" (Sheppard, 1989, p. 145). Most try to blend in—that is, present a feminine appearance but behave in a businesslike (stereotypically masculine) manner.

Gutek's (1989) literature review addresses another dimension of women's organizational reality. Studies show that, in general, women are associated with the status of sex object—with being (regardless of context) sexual beings who "naturally" evoke sexual overtures from men:

In a 32-nation study of sex stereotypes, the characteristics of sexy, affectionate and attractive were associated with femaleness. . . . *There is no strongly held comparable belief about men.* . . . The stereotype of men revolves around the dimension of competence and activity. It includes the belief that men are rational, analytic, assertive, tough, good at maths [sic] and science, competitive, and make good leaders . . . the perfect picture of asexuality. (Gutek, 1989, pp. 59-60)

Thus women in organizations have the additional problem of trying to appear feminine without triggering "natural" sexual reactions in men. If they do trigger such responses, women rather than men are customarily assumed to be at fault.

Culturally feminine characteristics do not fit the Weberian model of bureaucratic organization, which emphasizes instrumental rationality and official relations and excludes feeling. Pringle (1989) argues that Weber's idea of rationality, because it depends on excluding the personal, the sexual, and the feminine, can be read as a gloss on masculinity. She suggests that, although Weber saw the bureaucratic order of the modern world as a replacement for traditional patriarchy, one can see bureaucracy instead as a new form of patriarchy: "The apparent neutrality of rules and goals disguises the class and gender interests" that bureaucracy serves (Pringle, 1989, p. 161). Although obviously no actual bureaucracy fits Weber's ideal type exactly, our commonsense understanding of what an organization is supposed to be—a rational instrument for the efficient accomplishment of objectives—makes sexual emotion a taboo; as the people whose sex in organizations is problematic, women become associated with that which is forbidden, hence denied. Milwid (1990), for example, notes that both men and women professionals in organizations seek to deny the existence of sexual harassment. Nevertheless her research suggested that such incidents are widespread and that most go unreported, frequently because women are apt to blame themselves when men at work make overtures. Hale and Kelly (1989) report that a 1981 study by the Merit Systems Protection Board found that 48% of female federal employees had experienced sexual harassment, with "severe" harassment, such as pressure for sexual favors, twice as common as "less severe" (jokes, suggestive remarks).

Wells's (1973) study of the *covert power* of gender in organizations expresses the hidden sexual dimension of organizational reality in terms of the double bind women's presence places on men:

> If [the male manager] accepts women as managers, he has to accept as OK-for-a-manager the emotions he has repressed in himself; if he accepts the prescribed unemotional manager's role, he can't accept women (the feminine) as managers. . . .
> The male role requires that women be taken care of, not fought. So, many men feel locked into another double-bind: If he's a man as prescribed, he cannot relate to a women on an equal (male) basis; if he's his own person, relating as an equal to a women, he risks being seen by other men as "not much of a man"—or manager either. (p. 61)

Like women, then, men have to repress or deny aspects of themselves to function in organizations. Ferguson (1984) argues that the fact that most organizational men are in subordinate positions within the hierarchical structure of the bureaucracy requires them to behave in ways that outside the organization would be considered stereotypically feminine: For example, in general, men in organizations must cater to their superiors, avoid confrontation with them, and become sensitive to their idiosyncrasies. Their interest in being seen as real men, however, works to keep them from perceiving the prototypical femininity of their behavior. Kanter (1977) suggests that what looks like preference for masculinity in organizations is actually preference for power and that leadership styles are correlated not with gender but with the power of the position a particular leader holds. In her view, for example, the bossiness of women supervisors about which both male and female employees complain is not a feminine trait but the behavior of someone who has significant responsibility but little real power. Because in actuality most top leaders in organizations are men, however, organizational members continue to associate effective leadership with masculinity and to assume that a woman's problematic behavior has to do with her gender rather than her subordinate place in the structure or the power dynamics of the organization.[3]

Perhaps the most undeniable aspect of women's different organizational reality is their continued lack of access to high-ranking positions. More than a century after they took their first government jobs, women still constitute only a small fraction of the personnel in top civil service jobs (in the federal government in 1987, 6.9% of those in grades 16 to 18 were women), a circumstance increasingly being interpreted in terms of a *glass ceiling* that in subtle but effective fashion bars women from the most powerful strata of both public and profit-making organizations. In the economy generally, as Fierman (1990) notes, women now make up 40% of managers and administrators, but less than 0.5% of the more than 4,000 highest paid directors and officers of America's 1,000 largest companies. The influence of gender on the makeup of top corporate echelons is compounded by the effect of race. The author of a 1988 study comments:

> For white males, on average, 1 out of every 21 who enters a major corporation makes it to officer level within that corporation. For white females, the statistics are 1 out of every 136. For men of color, the ratio is 1 out of every 42. For women of color, there are no ratios, because in mid-1986, when we conducted the survey, we could not locate a woman of color at officer level within a major corporation. (quoted in Kelly, 1991, pp. 29-30)

In comparison, in 1990, minority women constituted 5.1% of top state and local government managers ("Few Women," 1992, p. A8).

Analysts attribute statistics on women's underrepresentation among organizational leaders in part to men's difficulty in reconciling organizational requirements with their personal views of women. Fierman (1990) reports that one executive search firm partner assessed the situation this way:

> Corporate males still don't know how to deal with women. They are afraid to yell at them or to give them negative feedback. It's as though they think they are yelling at their mothers or their wives. Men often worry women will run from the room in tears, or worse yet, yell back. (p. 41)

A 1984 literature review by Van Fleet and Saurage found that "public administration professionals still hold a substantially lower perception of female managerial ability than do those with other training" (quoted in Hale & Kelly, 1989, p. 27).

A Labor Department study, released in August 1991, of nine randomly selected *Fortune* 500 companies receiving federal contracts found barriers to women's advancement at lower management levels than anticipated. The situation for minorities was found to be worse than that for women—that is, white women. The study concluded that the glass ceiling exists (one feminist leader characterized the study as a waste of money for telling us what we already know). Labor Secretary Martin declined to interpret the findings as evidence of discrimination (Lawlor, 1991). One journalist interpreted the glass ceiling found in the study as support for a *neofeminist* argument that it is pointless for women to seek equality in a system in which men have made the rules. Instead, they should remodel the workplace along less hierarchical, more feminine lines (Saltzmann, 1991). Others, however, are likely to advocate the need to redouble efforts to strengthen affirmative action and pay equity policies.

One observer hypothesizes that as more women become conscious of the material realities of their organizational lives their discontent will rise (Laws, 1976); whether that discontent will simply lead to apathy in the face of seemingly insurmountable barriers or can be turned to more positive change efforts is an open question. For now, it is enough to note the need for theorists to rethink their conceptual models of bureaucratic hierarchy to include the existence of the glass ceiling, which appears to be as obdurate an aspect of bureaucratic structure as those that have received greater attention in the literature.

Standard organizational and professional career patterns and personnel policies depend on the existence of someone (that is, a wife) who takes care of household and child-care responsibilities. The 56 million women in the labor force, attempting to shoulder their domestic obligations and hold down paid jobs at the same time, work a double shift that is another factor in their different organizational reality. Because the American political economy counts on women as a group to handle these societal necessities irrespective of their individual inclination to do so, the arrangement constitutes oppression of women. Those who doubt the structural nature of women's disproportionate domestic burden should contemplate what would happen to organizational routines if one day all married employed women—or those unemployed because their small children "need someone at home"—

freely decided that they would no longer bear more than half the responsibility for housework and child care. Working women's double shift not only takes its toll in 18-hour days and stress-related illness; it also makes it difficult for women to meet employer expectations that family responsibilities will not interfere with work obligations and thus to keep up with (or get on) the fast track to the upper echelons of the organization. These tensions, or their prospect, in fact lead many women to deal with the double burden of job and family responsibilities by rejecting marriage and childbearing. Hale and Kelly's (1989) survey of public employees in Arizona, California, Utah, and Texas found that the living situations and domestic responsibilities of the male and female respondents were significantly different:

> Women are more likely to be divorced or never married, to be living alone, and without dependents. . . . Women are more likely than men to regard childbearing, child rearing, and household tasks as having interfered with their careers and . . . many apparently have resolved the traditional public/private role conflicts they face by not having a traditional family life. These women have not solved the historic dilemma of private/public role conflict; they have avoided it. Domestic responsibilities appear to constrain the career development of women more than men. (p. 144)

King (1992) found a similar pattern in her study of state managers in Colorado: 88% of the men in her sample were married in contrast to 59% of the women. Hale and Kelly (1989) also note that despite the fact that the women in their study had changed jobs within the bureaucracy at a faster rate and at younger ages than male respondents, they were still paid from $3,000 to $5,000 less than the men and on average supervised fewer employees.

Many women's life circumstances, of course, are such that they can afford little thought even of trying to get on the fast track. Also, as Andolsen (1986) observes, historically women of color have borne the burden of the double shift much longer than middle-class white women.

Sherley Williams calls the equal sharing of family responsibilities between men and women "the great revolution that never happened" (quoted in Okin, 1989, p. 4). Studies show that women still do about 70% of household tasks and working wives devote twice as much time to them as employed husbands. Men who are married to working women do only about 1.4 hours a week more housework than other husbands. A disproportionate amount of male domestic work involves relatively enjoyable pursuits like playing with the children (Rhode, 1988, p. 1183; see also Hochschild, 1989). Okin (1989) argues that during their developing years women "are set up for vulnerability" to exploitation in the marital relationship because they internalize society's expectation that they will be the primary child rearers (p. 138). Okin says that because the world of business (I would add government) is still structured around the assumption that employees are people who have wives at home and can thus work full time (or more), "to the extent that wives work part-time or intermittently, their own career potential atrophies" (p. 156). Okin (1989) holds that "the major reason that husbands and other heterosexual men living with wage-working women are not doing more housework is that *they do not want to, and are able, to a very large extent, to enforce their wills*" (p. 153). Okin suggests that the life circumstances—hence the career dynamics—of many women have been worsened by the trend in recent years toward treating men and women as equals before the law; for example, in the first year after divorce, the living standard of divorced men rises by 42% while that of divorced women falls by 73% (Leonore Weitzman, quoted in Okin, 1989, p. 161).

Thus, because gender stereotypes make women anomalies in the organizational context and because they suffer under economic arrangements that shore up accepted bureaucratic practices, women's organizational reality is significantly different from men's. On the one hand, they do not "fit" well within organizations, government or business; on the other hand, the standard procedures of these same organizations depend on them to provide support for the careers of male managers by shouldering not only a disproportionate share of domestic responsibilities but also much of the routine, poorly paid, lower-level organizational work. Far more women experience organizational reality, in the administrative state and in corporations, as data entry clerks, secretaries, bookkeepers, and maintenance workers than as vice presidents or bureau chiefs. Lewis calls clerical work the "quintessential female occupation" in the federal civil service. He notes that in 1982 approximately 49% of female federal employees were clerical workers and 85% of federal clerical workers were women (quoted in Hale & Kelly, 1989, p. 12). In addition, Hale and Kelly point out, in both state and federal governments career ladders for female-dominated positions have lower entry levels, less mobility across grade levels, and lower top levels. As Fierman (1990) observes, "by the year 2000 women will make up nearly one-half the labor force. But it won't be the top half" (p. 40). Most women develop their view of the organization sitting in the clerical bull pen at the bottom of the bureaucratic pyramid and/or dashing back and forth between home and work in a desperate effort to meet clashing expectations.

WOMEN AND THE ADMINISTRATIVE STATE

Most of the observations one can make about women's organizational reality apply equally whether the organization in question is public or private. But as many public administration theorists are fond of noting, public and business organizations are alike in all unimportant respects. In light of the research presented above, we would have to object that perhaps not *all* the ways in which governmental and business organizations are alike are unimportant. It remains true, however, that the differences between them are significant. Yet those that have to do with women and the peculiarities of their place in the political economy are rarely if ever taken into account in defenses of the administrative state.

The prevailing view of the uniqueness of public organizations is tied to the recognition of public administration as a form of governance, a view contemporary theorists owe to Waldo's (1948) introduction of the administrative state into the literature. The administrative state has received a good deal of attention (e.g., Kass & Catron, 1990; Perry, 1989; Rohr, 1986; Wamsley et al., 1990), and the legitimation literature of public administration treats bureaucratic decision making as in need of justification precisely because it constitutes a form of governance. Perhaps because work along these lines has had to cope with a tradition of *statelessness* in American political thought (Skowronek, 1982; Stillman, 1991), many of the implications of the concept of administrative state have been imperfectly explored. For example, Van Riper's (1983) widely cited list of characteristics of the administrative state includes none that frankly acknowledges politics, let alone power, as defining characteristics of a state.

To consider the place of women in the administrative state, we need a somewhat more nuanced understanding of the state than it frequently receives in public administration literature. According to Poggi (1990), the modern state is one manifestation of a more general trend toward the institutionalization of power, that is, toward a form of power that is depersonalized, formalized in law, and integrated into the greater social whole by means of a sense of nationhood or citizenship. Although the modern state is a complex assortment of organs, all its activities (except for a few momentous decisions) consist of directives of varying specificity and their implementation; these are made and carried out by a hierarchy of offices, whose holders have mastered knowledge of applicable laws and the intellectual techniques for interpreting them—who are, in fact, administrators exercising discretionary power.

The state asserts monopoly over "the business of rule," or the giving of commands (Poggi, 1978, p. 1), a function that in liberal pluralism is thought to distinguish it from the rest of society. Despite the interdependence of government and business obvious to the greenest student of political economy, liberal definitions of the state insist on maintaining the state's clear boundaries, in order to reserve a space of liberty for individual preferences and actions. Yet as Mitchell (1991) observes, "producing and maintaining the distinction between state and society is itself a mechanism that generates resources of power" (p. 90). He argues that contemporary politics does not consist of policy formation on one side of the divide and policy impact on the other, but of "the producing and reproducing of this line of difference" (Mitchell, 1991, p. 95). This critical perspective calls into question the obvious energy that is expended on maintaining the separation between state and society: Interest in continuance of the barrier, at least at a theoretic level, becomes the appropriate target of scrutiny rather than an accepted assumption.

Applying this thinking to public administration—that is, interrogating the insistence on a phenomenon called the *administrative state* wholly separate from something called *the private sphere*—we would have to ask what is obscured as a result of constructing and defending this firm boundary. The public-private distinction has served historically to maintain the perception that there is a clear line between government and business and to justify a realm in which "man" is protected from government interference in his activities. At the same time the public-private dichotomy has been used to distinguish the household from *both* government and business activities. Neither distinction has served women well; rather both have obscured women's needs and made them theoretical anomalies. The terms in which the administrative state's legitimacy is defended bring these incongruities into clearer focus.

Much of the recent attention paid in the literature to the administrative state comes from the need to combat bureaucrat bashing by making what public administrators do seem special. Theorists are motivated to portray the administrative state as distinctive in order to improve the bureaucrat's image—to reduce the danger that public administrators will be seen simply as business managers without profits (and judged in such terms, pitiful creatures indeed). I want to suggest, however, that regardless of intentions one of the major functions of a clear boundary around the administrative state is to obscure both its structural dependence on women's domestic work and its reach into the most private aspects of women's lives.

Since ancient times political philosophers have glorified the state by contrasting it with the household. Aristotle praised the *polis* on the basis of its self-sufficiency; in his view, because man's [*sic*] nature is political, the *polis* is higher in the overall scheme of things than household activities necessary to human existence (Aristotle, 1981). The essence of politics, then, is to rise above necessity (Brown, 1988). A similar distinction was made by Machiavelli, who conceived of statecraft as the mastery of fate: Political virtue (from *vir*, "man") consists in achieving control over matter (from *mater*, "mother")—over an explicitly female *fortuna* (Pitkin, 1984). Here again, affairs of state are seen as separate from and superior to the concerns assigned to women. Liberal philosophy also drew a sharp line, this time between the "natural" authority of the male in the family and political authority, which rests on consent. For Locke, the chief end of government was to protect individual property rights, but to avoid extending these rights to women and thus threatening the entire social order he postulated the natural inferiority of women based on the burdens of childbearing (Clark, 1979). Rousseau's ideal state is dependent on the existence of the home as a refuge, to which the male citizen can retreat from the demands of public life to have his physical and emotional needs met by his woman (Lange, 1979).

The revolutionary eras in America and France offer examples of the deliberate ordering of the public sphere at the expense of women. In America, founding father John Adams replied with a verbal pat on the head to his wife Abigail's admonition to "remember the ladies" when designing the new government. But Abigail Adams knew that she had raised a serious and potentially threatening question. To a male colleague, John Adams voiced his anxieties:

> How . . . does the right arise in the majority to govern the minority, against their will? Whence arises the right of the men to govern the women, without their consent? . . . You will say, because their delicacy renders them unfit for practice and experience in the great business of life . . . as well as the arduous cares of state. . . . True. But will not these reasons apply to others? Depend upon it, Sir, it is dangerous to open so fruitful a source of controversy. . . . New claims will arise; women will demand a vote; . . . and every man who has not a farthing, will demand an equal voice with any other, in all acts of state. (quoted in Rossi, 1973, pp. 10-15)

Landes's (1988) study of the development of public space in prerevolutionary France offers another clear example of the deliberate ordering of public and domestic spheres at the expense of women. Under monarchical rule in 18th-century France, the institution of the *salon* offered the only space where men and women could converse about public affairs. Hosted by women, *salons* provided the means whereby men learned the style, language, and art necessary to operate in public and served as the arena within which important issues were discussed. Landes argues that men, "feminized" by the king's absolute power, came to see women's role in the political dialogue of the *salons* as analogous to the king's monopoly over the terms of political life. Over time, men saw the silencing of women and their banishment from a reconstituted public space as necessary elements in the challenge to monarchy.

Landes (1988) suggests that, once expelled so a masculine public sphere can be constructed, women violate the code of political behavior when they attempt to reshape public language in order to make it possible to express certain of their issues. Seen, because of their exclusion from public life, as unutterably different, women can only give voice to what are regarded as partial concerns rather than join in what men believe to be the universal discourse of the public sphere—what we in public administration now call *public-interested dialogue*. One small but significant indication of the masculinity of the public sphere and its discourse is that, in contrast to the respect accorded *public man*, since time immemorial the term *public woman* has had the connotation "prostitute."

Reconstructing our idea of the public—hence of the administrative state—involves questioning the boundaries we have drawn around it, which defined women out and now leave them struggling with whether to try to "become men" in order to participate. For one thing, we must begin to question the uniqueness of some of the state's purported characteristics. For example, Franzway, Court, and Connell (1989) observe that the state is neither the only institutionalization of power nor even its only *legitimate* holder. The family is also a locus of power relations, and parents exercise legitimate force (short of real injury) on their children. They also note that, far from holding itself aloof from private issues, the administrative state develops and implements policies, such as those on divorce, birth control, and abortion, that affect our most intimate behaviors. Epstein (1988) argues that the terms of many public policies, such as protective labor laws and the prohibition on women serving in combat, far from simply *reflecting* gender distinctions in society, actually maintain and reinforce them, including ones that disadvantage women. Franzway et al. (1989) note:

> The state is not "outside" society. . . . Gender relations form a large-scale structure, embracing all social institutions in particular ways. . . . The state participates in this dynamic on the same footing as any other institution (for instance reflecting the overall changes in women's employment in the last generation). . . . The state sets limits to the use of violence, protects property, criminalises stigmatized sexuality, embodies masculine hierarchy. . . . The state takes a prominent part in constituting gender categories (the homosexual, the prostitute, the housewife, the family man) and regulating the relationships among them by policy and policing. (p. 52)

Like other liberalist views of the state, public administration's defense of the administrative state depends on the state's faithful adherence to the public interest, broadly understood. From this perspective, the thing that sets public administrators apart is their commitment to the common good ahead of their own self-interests. Such an understanding turns real (not abstract) public administrators into a class set apart from the common people by its ability to rise above self-interest into the realm of universalized concerns. While contemporary theorists have ostensibly discarded Wilson's politics-administration dichotomy and acknowledged the inherently political character of bureaucrats' discretionary judgments, most have yet to consider whether a pursuit that so assiduously denies the gender (as well as race and class) dynamics of its development can be trusted to be able to tell the partial from the universal. Although the occasional theorist addresses the administrative state's role in tending the dynamics of advanced capitalism and most acknowledge its unavoidable entanglement in interest group politics, its implication in the construction and maintenance of gender distinctions—most of which are invidious for women—has yet to be explored. Evidently, where *sexual* politics are concerned, the politics-administration dichotomy still guides public administration theory.

CONCLUSION

This chapter presented some dimensions of women's realities in the world of practice that public administration theory has ignored. While public administration scholars overwhelmingly acknowledge that the field is an applied one and debate ways of making their research more responsive to the needs of practitioners, one aspect of the real world of public administration has gone perpetually unnoticed—the dynamics of gender. Since they first entered government work in 1861, women's experience of life in public agencies has been materially different from men's. Women have been paid less, done a disproportionate share of the routine work, struggled with the question of how to accommodate them-

selves to organizational practices defined by men, brooded over how to turn aside men's advances without losing their jobs, and fought to balance work demands with what was expected of them on the domestic front. Those who have made it to the middle ranks find themselves bumping up against a glass ceiling that keeps a disproportionate number of women from top positions.

Since ancient times, men have defined the nature of public life in contrast to the pursuits of women. Despite the fact that no one could live for very long—and certainly conversations in the *polis* would quickly grind to a halt—without shelter, hot meals, clothing, nurturance, and the raising of the young, historically men have seen this "women's work" as beneath them; while they have depended on women, and still do, to perform these necessary tasks, they have asserted their own greater fitness to govern, that is, to give binding answers to questions of the common good. Through the ages men have been able to understand the significance and appreciate the worth of what they do by comparing it with what they did not do—in other words, with what women did. At the same time, they have not left sex roles to childhood socialization alone: Through the activities of the state (in more recent times, the administrative state) they have exerted restrictions over women's options on the basis merely of their sex.

Subsequent chapters explore further some of the ramifications of women's different organizational reality, our failure to take it into account in constructing defenses of administrative governance, and its role in images of expertise, leadership, and virtue. Here I have simply introduced a number of the gender-based material characteristics of the administrative state to suggest that theorists' recognition of them is long overdue.

NOTES

1. Wilson defended the segregation of African-American civil servants as a move to protect them from harassment. In response to a letter of protest from Oswald Garrison Villard, New York *Evening Post* editor and grandson of abolitionist William Lloyd Garrison, Wilson commented:

It is true that the segregation of the colored employees in the several departments was begun upon the initiative and at the suggestion of several of the heads of departments, but as much in the interest of the negroes as for any other reason, with the approval of some of the most influential negroes I know, and with the idea that the friction, or rather the discontent and uneasiness, which had prevailed in many of the departments would thereby be removed. . . . My own feeling is, by putting certain bureaus and sections of the service in the charge of negroes we are rendering them more safe in their possession of office and less likely to be discriminated against. (Baker, 1931/1968, p. 221)

2. Among state and local employees in 1987, approximately 73% received free parking as a benefit but only 2% got child care (Peterson, 1992).

3. According to Powell (1988), research indicates that the longer men work with women peers the less likely they are to interpret their behavior in terms of gender stereotypes.

3

"Sharpening a Knife Cleverly":
The Dilemma of Expertise

One of the most pervasive themes in defenses of the administrative state is the expertise of public administrators. Practitioners and scholars alike argue that competence in the art of administrative governance entitles public administrators to a certain measure of power in the exercise of their discretion. Debate centers not on this fundamental claim but on relatively secondary questions like the specific nature of the expertise, or whether it makes sense logically or strategically to consider public administration a profession.

For example, Morgan (1990) asks "What particular competence do and/or should public administrators possess in their exercise of [discretionary] authority?" rather than "Does expertise justify authority?" (p. 70). Gawthrop (1984) wonders whether the "craft of management" can revivify the "art of government" (p. 106). He acknowledges that giving administrators this responsibility is controversial, but in his view it "can only be effectively discharged by permanent, career civil servants" (p. 106). The "Blacksburg Manifesto" argues that whether or not we call public administration a profession, what really matters is recognition of its "truly distinctive claim to status . . . [that is,] a claim of competence in the maintenance of (1) the Agency Perspective; (2) the broadest possible public interest; and (3) the constitutional governance process" (Wamsley et al., 1990, pp. 47, 39). Pugh (1989) observes— in a piece generally critical of professional status for public administration—that "The reconciliation of traditional democratic values and the need for competent expertise in the governance process is a fundamental puzzle piece in public administration's search for reasonableness" (p. 5). Cigler (1990) sees a "paradox of professionalization" in public administration: The more we try to professionalize, the lower we sink in public esteem. Nevertheless, she calls on public servants to "be more proactive in lobbying for the broad public interest" rather than urging them to question the extent to which competence entitles them to power (p. 649).

While some writers in this vein maintain a certain level of skepticism about the virtues of professional status for public administration, others seek to mold the idea of professionalism in order to put it to the service of public administration's need for legitimacy. For example, Stever (1988, pp. 171ff.) rejects the traditional professional model on the grounds that public administrators cannot claim exclusive control over their work but, nevertheless, offers a strategy for the professionalization of public administration, a project that in his view includes recognition of its "cruciality" and the acquisition of a "mystique." Nalbandian (1990) emphasizes the "rational and analytic problem-solving orientation" of local government professionals, without which they seem "hardly distinguishable from the politician" (p. 659). Kearney and Sinha (1988) present perhaps the most ardent recent defense of professional status for public administration: "[We agree] with such notables as Aristotle, John Stuart Mill, Woodrow Wilson, and Max Weber that the preservation of a democratic system depends upon the competence of experts in government. . . . The expanded role of the professional administrator has benefitted bureaucratic responsiveness" (p. 571).

The substance of the public administrator's expertise is, in theory, wide ranging. It appears to include specialized (scientific, technical, and/or managerial) knowledge, analytical and problem-solving skills, the ability to see the longer view and the bigger picture, and other cognitive abilities but also normative ones as well, such as an especially acute understanding of the constitutional governance process or what constitutes the public interest in particular situations. Chapter 5 considers normative abilities in its discussion of the public administrator's virtue; here I deal with the question of technical and managerial expertise, especially as it relates to the issue of professionalism.

There are four aspects of professional expertise in public administration that contain gender dilemmas: its claim of scientific objectivity, its quest for autonomy, the hierarchical nature of the authority it seeks, and its implicit norm of brotherhood. In considering these points, my aim is to show that each one depends on the assertion of culturally masculine qualities and values and the disparagement of feminine ones and assumes a social order that disadvantages women. I suggest that current images of expertise are problematic because they encourage us to perceive the practice of public administration in ways that, though we tend to see them as neutral or universal, are actually gender biased and support concrete discrimination against women. The chapter concludes with a brief discussion of the paradoxes women and the profession as a whole face as a result of arguments for public administration's legitimacy based on seeing administrators as experts.

OBJECTIVE EXPERTISE

Objectivity and neutrality have been cited ever since Woodrow Wilson and Frank Goodnow as major bases for the legitimacy of administrative experts in a constitutional democracy. In order to "run a constitution," Wilson (1887/1978) argued, the "eminently practical science of [public] administration" must look to wherever expert methods are practiced, whether it be the business world or European monarchy (p. 16). The reason we need not worry about borrowing techniques from these seemingly alien realms is because expert methods themselves are neutral. In a famous metaphor, Wilson maintains:

If I see a murderous fellow sharpening a knife cleverly, I can borrow his way of sharpening the knife without borrowing his probable intention to commit murder with it; and so, if I see a monarchist dyed in the wool managing a public bureau well, I can learn his business methods without changing one of my republican spots. (p. 16)

Wilson's argument is only the most familiar expression of a theme that pervaded the Progressive reform movement: the need to rescue governance from bias, corruption, and bossism—the waste, fraud, and abuse of that era—by turning it over to neutral experts. In Wilson's thought, the problem of reform went beyond throwing the rascals out to ensuring the authority of scientific administrative expertise in a democratic system; the solution was to establish a dichotomy between administration and politics. Administrative methods could be acquired from any source as long as their application was unbiased—free from partisan politics. Goodnow (1900/1981) made the dichotomy even more explicit: The only thing that would protect the public's will from being corrupted in practice was to keep its execution by administrators completely separate from its expression, which belonged in the legislature.

The politics-administration dichotomy, with its reliance on neutrality, justified administrative governance for more than half a century, but fell from grace when the exigencies of carrying out the war effort during the 1940s made it clear that administration and politics were inextricably intertwined—or so goes the conventional wisdom regarding the intellectual history of the field. In actuality, although most observers consider the idea of neutrality out of date, it is still very much with us in the common assumption that in practice expert administrators can rise above their own beliefs and the political fray to fix their sights on the public interest, broadly conceived. But as Harold Seidman has suggested, if the 1937 report of the President's Commission on Administrative Management (the Brownlow Commission) marked the "high noon" of the politics-administration orthodoxy, then someone "apparently stopped the clock" (quoted in Rosenbloom, 1987, p. 78). Like the reform thinkers of a century ago, present-day theorists continue to see public administrators as, at least ideally, objective experts able to perform detached analyses of situations and to weigh claims impartially. Rosenbloom (1987) notes the durability of this "administrative culture," with its insistent search for, and claims of, efficiency, economy, science, facts, and management. These persistent assumptions about the objectivity and neutrality of expertise are fraught with gender contradictions. One of the most enduring patterns in Western thought has been to link the achievement of supposedly unbiased knowledge with masculinity, while tying "nature," or that which is known, to the female. Francis Bacon conceived of the scientific method as the frank seduction of feminine nature: "I am come in very truth leading to you Nature with all her children to bind her to your service and make her your slave. . . . For you have but to follow and as it were hound nature in her wanderings" (quoted in Keller, 1985, p. 36).[1] The scientific method and its fruits do not "merely exert a gentle guidance over nature's course; they have the power to conquer and subdue her, to shake her to her foundations. . . . Neither ought a man to make scruple of entering and penetrating into those holes and corners, when the inquisition of truth is its whole object" (quoted in Harding, 1986, p. 116). While nature has been seen as a female to be hounded and subdued, the seeker after knowledge, at least since Descartes, is a *separated self* who remains detached in order to know and control. Knowledge requires disconnection from the disorderly, feminine field of observation to avoid muddying the results with bias (Bordo, 1987). The cultural masculinity of this mode of knowing, which aims to prevent contamination by removing from the research process all traces of the individual scientist, is implied in the characterization of its products as *hard data*, as distinct from the *soft data* acquired by interactive procedures such as interviewing or participant observation. As Keller (1985) argues, the preference for hard over soft data is a reflection of cultural preference for the masculine over the feminine as well as men's historical predominance within science and the societies science serves.[2]

A number of feminist scholars argue that, because in Western society male children tend to equate self-development and maturity with the attainment of autonomy and separation from their mothers (Chodorow, 1978; Gilligan, 1982) and because men still largely remain in control of social processes, only knowledge gained by means of detachment from the field of observation is seen as qualifying for the term *scientific*—only *this* is *really* knowledge. According to Keller (1985), this narrow a view of the nature of knowledge could only prevail because historically in Western society (white, well-educated) men have set the requirements for knowledge development. Under such circumstances it became possible to universalize a set of norms that conformed to these men's ways of looking at the world. Over time the entire society came to see the specific as the universal and other ways of knowing as limited if not flawed in comparison.[3]

The idea of neutrality, which serves in political thought as the equivalent of objectivity, is a fundamental tenet of the classical liberalism that undergirds American government. To preserve individual freedom and equality, the liberal state must maintain neutrality with respect to individual preferences; the state serves simply as a referee, managing the process by which claimants compete. Yet, as feminist theorists have shown, this claim of neutrality dissolves when one focuses on the extent to which liberal thought—and the state that took shape in tandem with it—depends on women's continued exclusion from the public space where competition among political equals is supposed to take place. As Mary Astell put it in 1700, "If all Men are born free, how is it that all Women are born slaves?" (quoted in Jagger, 1983, p. 27).

While political theories that rationalized the existence of monarchy had not been inconsistent with the subordination of women, the liberal claim of individual freedom based on human rationality made women a problem for political philosophers; logic dictated either that women, as human beings, were rational and therefore possessed equal liberty with men or that despite being human they were somehow deficient in rationality and therefore deserved to be barred from public life. The typical way of overcoming this dilemma was to assert woman's equality in theory but defend her continued inequality in practice on instrumental grounds, such as the need to maintain the integrity of home and family. For example, Locke argued that although theoretically women are free to overcome their "natural limitations" their physical weakness justifies practices that subordinate them (Butler, 1978). Thus for women today it may be less easy than it is for men to see the liberal idea of the government's neutrality as unproblematic. The state has never been neutral on the subject of women—in fact, at the time when Wilson and Goodnow were urging administrative neutrality, women still could not vote. If Wilson, who was teaching at Bryn Mawr when he penned his famous essay, had listened to his students (all females) on the issue of suffrage instead of disdaining and patronizing them,[4] he might have been more cautious about concluding that "the weightier debates of constitutional principle" were "no longer of more immediate practical moment than questions of administration" (Wilson, 1887/1978, p. 4).

The viability of the idea of objective expertise depends heavily on sustaining confidence in reason's effectiveness as a means of acquiring knowledge. Numerous observers have suggested that the development of professions during the 19th century involved setting an exaggerated value on reason at the expense of the emotions. Bledstein (1976) notes that the heavy emphasis on rationality during this time stemmed from the anxiety of the middle-class man over the threat of failure to "prove himself tough-minded and vigilant—a man" and about "losing out to the competition and being compromised" (pp. 114-115). Haber's (1964) study of scientific management points out how faith in science introduced standards of disinterestedness and rigor into managerialism, with its interest in guidance and control of organizational processes. Ginszberg (1990) argues that the desire to professionalize social work made it necessary to discount the value of middle-class women's volunteer work on the basis that femininity was essentially irrational: "Increasingly, male values were viewed as necessary to control and limit a female effusion of emotion, sensibility, or passion; either those sensibilities would submit to law and system or they would become entirely ineffective, even dangerous" (p. 173).

Certainly, both men and women of the time saw feminine feelings as a threat to the impartiality of professional judgment, which was (and is) typically thought to depend on the exercise of dispassionate reason. Young (1987) explains that impartiality connotes "being able to see the whole," which means being able to "stand outside and above the situation," a move that can only be made by the decontextualized, separated self (pp. 60-61). The impartial reasoner aims to banish uncertainty by eliminating the specifics of situations; through detachment, which facilitates seeing all possible perspectives, the reasoner need not consult with real people. In addition, being impartial means being *ruled* by reason— in the sense not of simply having reasons but of reducing "objects of thought to a common measure, to universal laws" (p. 61). Such reason entails being unaffected by feelings; "only by expelling desire, affectivity and the body from reason can impartiality achieve its

unity" (p. 62). In contrast, decisions based on sympathetic understandings, on caring, are defined as sentimental.

The *passion for anonymity* that animated the Brownlow
Commission's ideal administrator appears to promise the impartiality—the impersonality—necessary to justify administrative power
by keeping it uncontaminated by politics. But as a practical matter, such anonymity becomes more difficult to sustain when administrators themselves become a more diverse group. Administrators can only maintain a posture of anonymity if their individual
identities can be counted on to have no effect on their actions. One
can only have a passion for anonymity if one is willing and able
to identify—at least in practice if not in one's heart—with accepted
agency viewpoints and methods, a move that is problematic for
people who have, until relatively recently, been restricted to the
margins of the bureaucracy or barred from it entirely. As women and
people of color infiltrate decision-making processes in public organizations, the assumption that everyone in the agency holds the same
norms in common becomes less dependable. In recognition of this,
theories of representative bureaucracy (for example Krislov, 1974),
which stress the hiring of personnel who reflect the demographics of
their jurisdictions, not only assume that people's viewpoints are
affected by their race, class, and gender but actually treat such
linkages as an asset in achieving bureaucratic responsiveness.

One might protest that no one in public administration any
longer advocates a passion for anonymity. But scholars continue to
justify administrative discretion on the basis that it represents the
agency perspective rather than that of any one individual. The
best-known argument is that of Wamsley and his colleagues (1990):
They have advocated recognizing agencies as "repositories
of . . . specialized knowledge, historical experience, time-tested wisdom, and most importantly, some degree of consensus as to the
public interest relevant to a particular societal function" (p. 37). And
so agencies undoubtedly are—but surely the point of the agency
perspective is that, by buying into it, an individual administrator
takes on the identity of the agency and in so doing reduces the risk
of idiosyncrasy in decision making. The individual becomes anonymous in the sense of serving as a reliable surrogate for the agency
as a whole. It would seem, however, that a coherent agency
perspective, particularly one with a historical dimension, would
have to have been shaped by the identities of the persons who

have comprised the agency over time. An agency with a mostly white middle-class male professional membership will find it easier to reach the common perspective to which the Blacksburg theorists look than could be the case once the agency membership becomes more diverse. The Blacksburg argument, despite its attempt to take situational factors seriously, falls into the same conceptual trap as the Brownlowian passion for anonymity, that is, it fails to consider both the partiality of a perspective developed by a narrow range of humanity and the impact of increasing public work force diversity on the continuing achievement of a shared point of view. I do not mean to suggest that a common frame of reference is impossible or that it might not be desirable; I do argue that the detachment from the body and from life experience required by a norm of objectivity leads theorists to overestimate the universality of certain values and approaches and the ease of developing a shared perspective. We will not attain a truly contextual understanding of public administrative practice until we open up what now passes for the agency perspective in practice and in theory to the views, values, and perceptions of *others* (nonwhite, nonmale) who are increasingly inside agencies where they were once mainly clients of them. If the agency perspective is to serve as a real alternative to administrative anonymity, we must examine the ways in which it is constructed and take into account the transformative potential of placing real, as distinguished from lip service, value on diversity.

PROFESSIONAL AUTONOMY

The culture of professionalism incarnated the radical idea of the independent democrat, a liberated person seeking to free the power of nature within every worldly sphere, a self-governing individual exercising his trained judgment in an open society. The Mid-Victorian as professional person strove to attain a level of autonomous individualism, a position of unchallenged authority heretofore unknown in American life.

Bledstein (1976, pp. 87-88)

Bledstein's study of the development of professionalism during the 19th century places appropriate stress on the notion of autonomy. Most treatments of professionalism in the sociological literature center around control over the content and conditions of work as a defining feature (e.g., Vollmer & Mills, 1966). Professional knowledge and its application in practice are said to be so specialized that no outsider is qualified to judge the competence of an individual practitioner or the profession as a whole. Professionals reserve the right to assess what work they are qualified to do as well as the right to police themselves. These rights are so central that groups of workers who reflect other definitive characteristics of professionalism (such as specialized knowledge or a commitment to service) but who lack autonomy in practice have been styled *semiprofessions* in the literature (Etzioni, 1969). In the present context, perhaps it is worth noting that the usual examples given in discussions of semiprofessions—social workers, nurses, and other so-called allied health personnel—are predominantly female occupations; this suggests that the ability to make an effective claim of professional autonomy is not unaffected by the gender dimensions of the groups in question.

As Mosher's (1968) classic discussion argued, the celebrated autonomy of the professional conflicts with the public administrator's obligation to be responsive to the public interest and to account for his or her actions to elected and politically appointed officials. Yet despite Mosher's suggestions, many of the current images of the public administrator continue to imply a high level of autonomy in practice. Rohr (1986) sees public administration as a balance wheel in the system of separated powers, weighing and choosing which of several masters (executive, legislative, or judicial) to obey in particular circumstances. Similarly, O'Leary and Wise (1991) argue that administrators may choose to cooperate with or resist particular court decisions according to their sense of whether executive branch prerogatives are being encroached on. As a group, public administration theorists worry more about instilling proper values in the hearts of administrators so that their power will be exercised wisely than about imposing limits on their autonomy.[5] Factors that act as limits on the autonomous exercise of administrative discretion, such as civil service regulations, requirements for citizen participation, or due process rules, are typically treated as impediments to administrative effectiveness—as red tape (e.g., Wilson, 1989).

The concern for effectiveness that animates arguments in favor of autonomy in the exercise of administrative discretion is of long standing. White's (1948) observation that the Federalists "had a deep fear of governmental impotence" makes the point in a manner that hints at its underlying masculinity (p. 510). Alexander Hamilton in particular strove to ensure that the federal chief executive would have enough power both to check the irrationality of the legislature and to be proactive and efficacious in the development and implementation of policy. Hamilton's concern for "energy" in the executive branch persists today in the administrator's assertion of the right to autonomy.

In recent literature this claim has sometimes taken the form of seeing the public administrator as *agent* of the people or of the public interest. Kass (1990) argues that in law the idea of agency grew out of the need to reduce the isolation that a political economy made up of unfettered individuals can produce, by conceiving of a way for them to act in one another's stead. The agent can work on behalf of others and still retain considerable personal and moral autonomy. Kass notes that "in earliest times, those who acted for others were normally family dependents or bound servants who, in a real sense, were mere extensions of a *pater familias*" (p. 115). Thus the idea of agent evolved in a direction that divested it (whether consciously or not) of the implicit powerlessness associated with women (*family dependents*) or lower-class people (*bound servants*). Wamsley's (1990) image of agency, while it reflects a similar emphasis on acting for others, emphasizes the agent's exertion of responsible power. Wamsley recognizes the tension inherent in two interpretations of agency: one in which the principal acts *through* the agent (equivalent to Kass's extension of the *pater familias*), the other in which the agent acts on behalf of the principal but not under specific orders. Though either agent could potentially achieve effectiveness, only the latter has autonomy. For Wamsley the public organization's need for purposive rationality tips the balance in favor of the agential administrator who has autonomy (is, in fact, a *helmsman*), yet he recognizes that the helmsman must still be subordinate to other institutions of government.

The scholarly struggle to develop an image of public administrative autonomy that entails a level of responsiveness sufficient for a representative government reflects a gender dilemma because of the associations we normally make between subordination and femininity, between autonomy and masculinity. The struggle to think of a way to embrace responsiveness, obedience to the popular will, and compliance with the legitimate dictates of other branches of government, without simultaneously embracing femininity, reflects the effort to retain the sense of separated selfhood—of agency—that is a central feature of our understanding of masculinity. Masculinity is embodied in the self, the knower, the actor, the subject, while the other, that which is known, that which is acted on, the object—these are feminine (De Beauvoir, 1961). As Young (1987) puts it:

> An essential part of the situation of being a woman is that of living the ever present possibility that one will be gazed upon as a mere body, as shape and flesh that presents itself as the potential object of another subject's intentions and manipulations, rather than as a living manifestation of action and intention. (p. 66)

The public administrator's self-image is of one who sees—but is also seen. In this respect, ironically, the public administrator is like De Beauvoir's woman: As humans, public administrators are subjects, but they are also objects of the gaze of their various masters (agency heads, the legislature, the courts, the people at large). Like women, public administrators must live this contradiction. The form taken by theories of administrative discretion suggest that assertions of autonomy entail unconscious denials of the femininity that lies beneath the image of the responsive administrator.[6]

THE HIERARCHY OF EXPERTISE

The assertion of autonomy is simultaneously a claim of authority, particularly when made within a political context. A number of writers on the Progressive era have commented on this element in the rise of the professional bureaucrat. For example, Skowronek (1982) suggests that the antiparty "good government" thrust of the new 19th-century professional class aimed to counteract efforts by party politicians to bar "the finest culture and highest intellectual power" from positions of influence (p. 43). Wiebe (1967) calls attention to how middle- and upper-class perceptions of societal complexity, fluidity, and disorder became the grounds for promoting the expert authority of the bureaucrat. Haber (1964) argues that the Progressive ideology of efficiency promised social harmony once those who were competent led society and conflicting purposes disappeared under the rule of "facts."

As Bledstein (1975) notes, "Far more than other types of societies, democratic ones required persuasive symbols of the credibility of authority" (pp. 123-124). Professionals in the 19th and early 20th centuries were able to achieve this credibility based on the prestige afforded them by their advanced education and by "appealing to the universality and objectivity of 'science.' " Thus Progressive leader Henry Lawrence Gantt could regard with disdain the "debating society theory of government." In his view: "True democracy is attained only when men are endowed with authority in proportion to their ability to use it efficiently and their willingness to promote the public good. Such men are natural leaders whom all will follow" (quoted in Haber, 1962, p. 48).

The scientific management movement furthered the idea of authoritative expertise; Taylor (1911) not only distinguished organizational thinking from doing but elevated the former to a position of clear control. He believed the ordinary workman incapable of understanding the science on which the systematization of work was to be based; therefore, efficiency would be served by putting the professional manager—the thinker—in charge of the organization of work, while workmen would fulfill their responsibility by carrying out the manager's directives.

To a considerable extent, assertions of professional authority were couched in terms that reduced those over whom authority would be exerted to a state of dependence. Frequently this was accomplished through a rhetoric of crisis, abnormality, and disaster. Thus, according to Bledstein (1975), "the culture of professionalism exploited the weakness of Americans—their fears of violent, sudden, catastrophic, and meaningless forces" (p. 102). In a period when the middle class perceived the world to be in danger of turning upside down, professionals reassured them, promising to have the expertise necessary to combat these threats, and thus encouraging "public attitudes of submission and passivity" (p. 104). Wiebe's (1967) characterization of the Progressive era as a "search for order" makes a similar point. Complexity—urbanization, industrialization, immigration, labor unrest—evoked widespread anxiety, but particularly among elites, who "reached out for mastery" to "quash all disorder" (pp. 76-77).

One can observe this impulse in the rhetoric of Woodrow Wilson's essay on the study of administration, which begins with the argument that expert administration is made necessary by complexity. Once, "the functions of government were simple, because life itself was simple." But now, "present complexities of trade and perplexities of commercial speculation . . . perennial discords between master and workman . . . assume . . . ominous proportions" (p. 4). The solution is, of course, the science of administration and a public will that is not "meddlesome." Present-day theorists make similar arguments for the need to facilitate the administrator's exercise of discretion. For example, Long (1981) argues that tendencies of political stalemate and policy drift in the rest of the government justify the public administrator's authoritative governance. In a polity of "opposing demands," Wildavsky (1990) wonders, "can we denigrate hierarchy . . . while still honoring public service? Can there be an effective bureaucracy without respect for authority?" (pp. xvii-xviii).

The professional authority-societal complexity dualism is deeply gendered. As I have discussed elsewhere (Stivers, 1992b), at least since the beginning of the early modern period, the complexity, mystery, or threat perceived in nature has been associated with women, probably because men perceived them as closer to nature as a result of their childbearing and child rearing responsibilities. The phenomenon of witchcraft is an example of disorder in nature symbolized as feminine (Merchant, 1980). The image of the masculine head of state controlling the unruly, archetypally feminine masses is a notable feature of Western political philosophy. For example, Machiavelli's body politic is a woman's body, its head a male head. The true prince renders the people "submissive, grateful, loyal" (Brown, 1988, pp. 87-88, 109-110). John Knox argued that the ruler (the head or mind) of the body politic must be a man, for women's rule would be monstrous (Merchant, 1980). From the feminist perspective, the persistence of this dualism represents the heroic masculine ego's projection of the psyche's inner complexity onto the world. The threat to the sense of authority and control must originate in the world and not from within the self. Young (1987) notes that this dichotomy is hierarchical rather than symmetrical: not only are self and world distinct but self assumes primacy over world.

The image of the public administrator as authoritative expert has troubling ramifications for three groups that in practice occupy the subordinated, feminized status of *other*. First, the expert administrator's translation of the life experiences and political claims of *clients* into depoliticized *needs* that can be handled bureaucratically turns clients from intentional agents capable of dealing with their predicaments meaningfully, if not unaided, into passive recipients of government services (Fraser, 1990). From the administrative perspective, the best client is one who follows advice, has no problems that do not fit the regulations, and is grateful for benefits received; in other words the desirable client, regardless of sex, has culturally feminine characteristics. Second, the hierarchical character of professionalism blocks the potential for genuine dialogue with *citizens*, whose opinions can more easily be discounted or dismissed because they are not considered expert. For the administrator, the best citizen is one who is decorative rather than substantive and who understands the citizen participation role as follower, supporter, and ratifier rather than as co-equal. Finally, professionalism's equation of merit with advanced education blocks the mobility of nonprofessional *workers* in the bureaucracy, who are disproportionately women and people of color (Allen, 1987), and by inhibiting perceptions of mutual interest hinders the formation of alliances among professional and nonprofessional women (Franzway et al., 1989). Thus the authority of professional expertise feminizes clients, citizens, and other workers—and I hope it is clear by now that *feminization* refers to a political rather than a biological condition.

Lane and Wolf's (1990) reference to secretarial workers (rare in the literature) reflects the implicit acceptance of professional authority in the way it ignores the gender dimensions of this observation:

> The clerical and administrative support staffs play an undervalued but essential role in the effective maintenance of the administrative processes of government. . . . It is this clerical staff that can be relied upon to know which person to call and what pitfall to avoid . . . [and]

is often the most reliable and complete repository for [agency] strengths, foibles, folkways, and sensitivities. . . . Unfortunately, these capacities are often tied to lower-status occupational positions, so their importance is overlooked and performance poorly rewarded. (p. 69)

In the process of chastising others for overlooking the importance of clerical workers, Lane and Wolf have evidently overlooked the fact that the secretarial staff is made up almost entirely of females—or, if they have noticed it, they evidently attach no significance to it. They deserve credit for pointing out the contribution that low-status and low-authority employees make to agency effectiveness; but without specific attention to gender, and the role it plays in keeping disproportionate numbers of female public employees in these ill-paid, low-power positions, the observation has a patronizing ring.

BROTHERHOOD

In a 1915 presentation to the precursor of the National Association of Social Workers, Abraham Flexner (whose report on medical education speeded the professionalization of the physician) commented: "A profession is a brotherhood. . . . Professional activities are so definite, so absorbing in interest, so rich in duties and responsibilities, that they completely engage their votaries. The social and personal lives of professional men and their families thus tend to organize around a professional nucleus" (quoted in Glazer & Slater, 1987, p. 175). Flexner's observation highlights an aspect of professionalism that has been little noted in the literature of public administration: that it is a subculture, a community, an association. Banding together in formal association originally meant to professionals the ability to set agreed-on standards of competence and codes of conduct, so as to protect the public (Lubove, 1965). But as every student of Selznick (1957) knows, the institutionalization of a social phenomenon like professionalism is not a neutral process of formal organization, but entails the establishment of values. As they come together, members of a profession take on a shared set of norms and a way of seeing the world in common. This professional culture sets them apart from the rest of society. Wiebe (1967) notes: "Identification by way of skills gave [Progressive era professionals] the deference of their neighbors. . . . The shared mysteries of a specialty allowed intimate communion even at long range" (p. 113).

The professional emphasis on like-mindedness runs the risk of expanding into exclusivity based on ascriptive characteristics rather than on learning. Historically, restricting entrance to people of similar race, gender, and class appeared to strengthen bonds of trust among members of professions and assured them that ideas could be shared easily in a style with which they all identified. While the professions have lifted formal restrictions based on race and gender, patterns of membership established under these rules have been slow in dissipating—even today, for instance, the continued existence of medical and dental societies oriented to African-Americans suggests that people of color do not perceive the mainstream societies as sufficiently hospitable to them. At any rate, professionals have a perennial tendency to promote their unique perspective, mystifying their subject matter to veil the intuition and guess work that inevitably supplement "scientific" judgment; exclusivity helps ensure that those who are uninitiated in the uncertainties of practice remain that way—that the "fabric of legitimacy" endures (Glazer & Slater, 1987, pp. 238-239).

But there is more to professional brotherhood than simply its resistance to diversity. As Flexner noted, professional work is expected to be all-absorbing; therefore, it requires a family willing to organize itself around the requirements of professional work and to provide the necessities of life that single-minded devotion to career leaves the professional no time to worry about. Laws (1976) calls this

> The myth of the heroic male professional . . . a model of work motivation which is used as the standard for assessing all other workers . . . . His work is the most important thing in his life. . . . [His] career is so demanding as to preclude other major commitments. . . . The heroic male professional sacrifices "selfish" concerns like personal and family life to the demands of his career. (p. 36)

Because the heroic male professional is an ideal type that sets the standard for performance, workers who refuse or cannot afford to "sacrifice selfish family concerns" are perceived to be less accomplished, less committed, less worthy of advancement. Because women still bear the brunt of a disproportionate amount of responsibility for family life as well as because most are still socialized to believe that family needs come before career success, they make up most of these "lesser" workers. Women who try to pursue a dual career of professional and domestic work find themselves pretending that they are single-mindedly focused on the office and that their children's problems never intrude on their organizational lives. When they indicate their inability to work evenings and weekends, bosses gradually come to perceive them as less dedicated or less hardworking than their male colleagues, and as a result they are passed over at promotion time.

Thus the term *brotherhood* is apt: Professional membership is problematic for women in a way that it is not in the case of men. To be professionals women must figure out how to close the gap between themselves and the perceived norms of membership— ideas about what a "real" member looks and acts like; they must also deal with much greater difficulty in attaining the level of devotion to work expected of members. In the current professional subculture, women are apt, no matter how much they struggle to learn the lingo, to continue to feel like aliens.

PROFESSIONALISM AND WOMEN

As a way of summarizing and reflecting back on the images of the public administrator as expert, let us consider the challenges faced by the female bureaucrat who aspires to the status of professional expert. As should be clear by now, my argument is that defending the legitimacy of public administrators on the basis of their competence is problematic because the image of the public administrator thus conceived privileges masculine characteristics while denigrating and/or suppressing feminine ones, and depends for its coherence on maintaining women in a position of inequality with respect to life chances and resources. There may be a way of thinking about competence that does not entail seeing traditionally feminine qualities as inferior and keeping women at a disadvantage; if there is, the problem is not using expertise per se as a basis for defending the legitimacy of public administration but rather the notion of expertise we use. To understand the difficulty fully, let us consider the impact on women in public administration of the questions raised above.

In general, the effect on women is one of dissonance between the status *woman* and the status *professional expert*. Professional administrators are expected to be technically expert, objective, and impartial; they are expected to merge without difficulty (or at least without audible demur) into their agency's perspective; they are expected to display autonomous authority in the exercise of discretionary judgments; they are expected to share a worldview and set of values with like-minded fellow members of the profession; and they are expected to regard their work as primary in their lives—to devote long hours and uninterrupted years to it and to put its demands ahead of personal concerns. Societal expectations of women are, in almost every respect, polar opposites. Women are expected to be good at sensing other people's feelings, at caring about them and nurturing them; in the agency setting (as we saw in chapter 2) they are perceived as different, even problematic; although hope of their continued submissiveness has dimmed, they are still expected to be responsive to men and in their heart of hearts to prefer marriage to a head of household over independence and autonomy; they are still widely seen as not authoritative and ill-suited to the exercise of authority; their values are perceived not only as different from men's but less worthy (Gilligan, 1982)—thus the extent of their professional like-mindedness is in question; and they are expected to put home and family ahead of (or at least equal to) career and to bear the brunt of household responsibilities.

Thus women who pursue careers as professional public administrators are faced with a dilemma—the fundamental dissonance between what is expected of them as women and what is expected of them as professional experts. As we have seen, it is not just that professional characteristics are culturally masculine but that in addition they give masculinity an advantage over femininity and depend on structural arrangements that make it difficult for women to meet professional expectations. Thus it is fraudulent to offer women an equal opportunity to pursue a public service career and rise through the ranks of the bureaucracy while at the same time the requirements and exemplary qualities for that sort of career remain inconsistent with what is expected of them as women.

To point out that a number of women have done it successfully is to miss the point. They have virtually never done it without constant effort to manage their femaleness on the job (tackling issues such as how to appear authoritative yet not masculine) and without continuing struggle to balance work and home responsibilities. While many men may also feel some distance between their sense of themselves and what the role of professional expert requires, they never have to choose between being experts and being seen as masculine, and rarely do they assume a level of household duties, routinely borne by women, that significantly interferes with job requirements (when they do, their careers suffer because their attitudes are seen as insufficiently professional).

Thus the arguments for competence as a basis for the legitimacy of public administration entail a logic and a set of societal arrangements in which women and women's qualities are at a disadvantage. In concluding this discussion, I want to emphasize that it is not only women but the profession as a whole that struggles with a paradox that has gender dimensions. I mentioned above that public administration's stress on autonomy, on not simply taking orders but instead using discretionary judgment, is a culturally masculine concern in tension with the stereotypically feminine obligation to be responsive. One could argue that other aspects of public administration's political role are similarly feminine—for example, the norm of service. At the level of cultural ideology, it is women who serve others while men are served; women unselfishly devote themselves to helping the unfortunate, while men pursue self-interest, albeit sometimes the enlightened variety. If what makes public administrators different from other experts is their responsibilities of service and of responsiveness, then as a group they too, like women, do not fit the professional role very well: Professionalism is too masculine for the feminine aspects of public administration. In this context, the effort to assert the worth of public administration in such terms as *professional, helmsman, agent, objective scientist,* and *anonymous expert* is an effort to acquire masculinity and repress femininity or project it outwards. In this sense, public administration is not only masculinist and patriarchal, it is in fundamental denial as to its own nature and conceptually and practically impoverished as a result. Women are not the only ones in public administration faced with a gender dilemma. Theorists may extol the virtues of the responsive, caring bureaucrat who serves the public interest, but the argument will face uphill sledding until we recognize that responsiveness, caring, and service are culturally feminine qualities and that, in public administration, we are ambivalent about them for that very reason.

NOTES

1. According to Adams (1991), Bacon asserted that we must put nature "to the rack to compel her to answer our questions." Similarly, Galileo spoke of a need in our investigations of nature to "commit a rape of the senses."

2. Harding (1986) notes that feminist criticism of the detached, masculine self bears striking resemblance to Africanist criticism of the individualistic European self.

3. For a more in-depth discussion of these views as they apply to public administration, see Stivers (1992b).

4. In his diary, Wilson complained: "Lecturing to young women of the present generation on the history and principles of politics is about as appropriate and profitable as would be lecturing to stone masons on the evolution of fashion in dress" (October 20, 1887, quoted in Bragdon, 1967, p. 143). Bragdon comments that Wilson did not believe in higher education for women. Wilson continued to oppose female suffrage until 1918, when militant suffragists embarrassed him by picketing the White House carrying placards with quotations from his League of Nations speeches, such as " 'Liberty for the world' but none at home."

5. In terms of the classic debate between Friedrich (1940/1984) and Finer (1941/1984) on this issue, Friedrich's position, that the ultimate rein on administrative power was the administrator's inner sense of responsibility to the public good, has been in the ascendancy for some time over Finer's insistence on concrete external checks—perhaps ever since the debate itself.

6. In a similar but class-based analysis, Derber (1983) suggests that salaried professionals forfeit the right to make decisions about work objectives while exacting from employers compensatory privileges like status and technical autonomy; thus their expertise is put to the service of goals they do not choose. Derber argues that the reluctance of bureaucratic professionals to examine the extent to which agency goals diverge from their own interests and values reflects an unconscious denial of the extent to which they have been proletarianized.

4

"Look Like a Lady, Act Like a Man":
The Dilemma of Leadership

Theorists frequently justify the exercise of administrative discretion on the basis that it fills a need for public leadership. The rationale is based on the nature of the American system of government and politics. Both scholars and practitioners tend to see this system as characterized by complexity, turbulence, and fragmented power, all of which hinder governance. The argument runs as follows: A federal system marked by separation of powers and checks and balances and a politics driven by the conflicting demands of competing interest groups not only keep power from coalescing but also make it difficult to govern. Under such conditions, there is a great need for stability and vision, for people who can see beyond the contention and roadblocks that plague immediate issues, develop strategies and long-range plans, keep things overall on some sort of coherent course, resist the political urge to sacrifice basic capacities for short-term gains, generate new ideas for dealing with persistent social problems—and who have enough authority and power to bring a modicum of order and rationality into the turbulent arena of government. Structurally, because the career civil service entails continuity, stability, and a broad purview of the overall system, it is the ideal place to look to for this guiding vision.

In chapter 3, I argued that public administration uses the fragmented nature of American government and politics to justify professional autonomy. Here I suggest that apparent complexity and political turmoil also serve as warrants for an argument that, as leaders who have the vision necessary to steer the ship of state and stewards of fundamental administrative capabilities, public administrators merit the respect of other governmental actors and the general public. This approach to justifying administrative discretion sees it as an organizational phenomenon, a form of management, whereas in the previous chapter we looked at it as a professional function.

The organizational perspective in public administration emphasizes success in attaining agency goals. For example, Doig and Hargrove's (1987) study of public sector leaders argues that "because fragmentation and decentralization create checks and balances that obstruct 'orderly' innovation, . . . there will be a need for talented men and women who can define new goals, build coalitions that knit together public and private interests, and carry out other entrepreneurial tasks required in this society of great diversity" (pp. 19-20). Exemplary administrative leaders, by means of vision, drive, and ambition, make their mark on agencies and society at large as they develop and husband organizational capacities. Doig (1988), drawing on the work of Joseph Schumpeter, describes this sort of leader as an entrepreneur: someone who is rational and egotistical, who has the "will to found a private kingdom . . . the impulse to fight, to prove oneself superior," and who is motivated by "the joy of creating, of getting things done, or simply of exercising one's energy and ingenuity" (p. 21). Terry (1990), on the other hand, is critical of the entrepreneurial leadership model but still accepts the importance of leadership. In his view, the desired leader is a conservator. Drawing on Barnard and Selznick, Terry argues that an administrative elite is necessary in order to preserve the "institutional integrity" of public organizations—that is, in order to "preserve organization as the instrument of action" (Barnard, quoted in Terry, 1990, p. 404) and to maintain the organization's "distinctive competence" (Selznick, quoted in Terry, 1990, p. 404). Thus, although Terry resists the entrepreneurial emphasis on making a proactive difference and on dominating others, by preserving their agencies' core competencies his administrators make their own sort of mark and clearly bear a leader's responsibility for promoting and carrying forward important societal values. Keller (1988) criticizes what he sees as an overemphasis in the literature on goal accomplishment, particularly what he sees as a decided stress on "skillful manipulation and buffering"; but he, too, ends by calling for effective constitutional manager-leaders (pp. 71-72).

Mitchell and Scott (1987) suggest that arguments justifying public administration based on the need for public sector leadership are quite powerful when linked, as they usually are at least implicitly, to the notion of professional expertise. Couched in terms that draw heavily on organizational theory developed largely in the context of private business, the leadership argument

> suggests that only a few have the skill and vision to lead and that these few dwell, as administrators, in interdependent public and private organizations. More importantly, administrators have the right to draw economic benefits from their organizations without suspicion of economic exploitation. They are receiving their just deserts for doing a job few could do. (Mitchell & Scott, 1987, p. 447)

The questions these arguments raise for the place of women in public administration have to do with the intellectual baggage and material circumstances that, though we are usually unaware of it, support images of leadership and thus shape our understanding. For example, we might first want to ask why the idea of leadership has a legitimating effect despite there being little unarguable evidence that the variable *leadership* actually has a clear impact on situations where it is thought to be important:

> Decades of academic analysis have given us more than 350 definitions of leadership. Literally thousands of empirical investigations of leaders have been conducted in the last seventy-five years alone, but no clear unequivocal understanding exists as to what distinguishes leaders from non-leaders. . . . Never have so many labored so long to say so little. (Bennis & Nanus, 1985, p. 4)

After all this research, the most we seem able to say is that leadership is partly a matter of personal qualities and partly contingent on the situation. Yet books, articles, and conference presentations continue to call for "better leadership" as the answer to the problems of public agencies. Leadership has become public administration's *phlogiston*—the mysterious substance that, prior to the discovery of oxygen, was believed to be the ingredient in substances that made them burn. Our continued reliance on such a vague concept suggests that its function is ideological, in two senses of the word. Leadership is an important cultural myth by which we make sense of and impart significance to organizational and political experience; in addition, leadership is an idea used to support and rationalize the continuation of existing political-economic, racial, and gender arrangements.

In what follows, I approach leadership as an image that works in the context of public agencies to maintain existing patterns of discrimination against women, particularly against women of color and working-class women. Images of organizational leadership in Western industrialized societies have been developed in situations dominated by white, professional men and therefore not surprisingly reflect the personal characteristics, worldviews, and values of those who historically have occupied leadership roles. The result is that those who are not white, male, or professional tend to fit—or, more accurately, tend to be perceived as fitting—the leadership image rather poorly. People who fail to qualify on two or three of these counts (for example a female of color who occupies a support staff position) are likely to have more difficulty moving into and occupying leadership status than those who fail to measure up on only one count.[1]

My consideration of the image of leadership begins by summarizing, based on the literature in public administration and business management, what leadership appears to mean to us in organizational life. The discussion critiques four images of leadership: the leader as visionary, one who has the enlarged understanding and insight necessary to guide public organizations; the leader as decision maker, one who can take charge and move the organization forward; the leader as symbol, one who influences and motivates followers; and the leader as definer of reality, one who tells or shows others the meaning of their work. I then review ideas about women leaders, both sexist stereotypes and the views of those who argue that because of their life experiences and values women tend to practice a more interactive, nurturant form of leadership than the mainstream one. Next I deal with women's leadership dilemma, that is, the fundamental conflict that exists between, on one hand, the leadership role and its organizational function, and on the other, feminine gender. I argue that the disparity between images of leadership and norms of femininity force women to struggle to reconcile conflicting demands—"look like a lady" versus "act like a man"—a struggle that men, whatever their personal views on leadership, are able to avoid. From this perspective, the optimism of the literature on the strengths and advantages of women's "different" leadership style—the view that as women become leaders they will change organizations—must be at least questioned. The chapter concludes with a few reflections on what this argument implies about the appropriateness of trying to legitimize public administration on the basis of its ability to provide public leadership.

A PORTRAIT OF THE LEADER

There are three important characteristics that may be crucial to successful innovative action carried out in the complex environment of the government office: a capacity to engage in systematic rational analysis; an ability to see new possibilities offered by the evolving historical situation; and a desire to "make a difference"—to throw one's energies and personal reputation into the fray in order to bring about changes.

Doig and Hargrove (1987, p. 11)

A successful organization, it has been said, requires three kinds of individuals: a dreamer, a businessman, and a son-of-a-bitch. In today's best leaders, these disparate qualities are merged.

Potts and Behr (1987, p. 201)

As these quotations illustrate, most discussions of leadership include a list of the leader's key qualities, and most feature the leader's vision, decision-making or take-charge capacities, and motivational and inspirational ability. Some also argue that we use leaders to help us find significance in what we do—literally, to tell us what our work means.

Let us begin our portrait of the organizational leader by considering the idea of vision. This theme runs through the public administration and business management literatures. Doig and Hargrove (1987) mention "an ability to see new possibilities." Bellavita (1986) suggests that leadership is "an organizational process made up of . . . a vision, . . . political support for the vision; people willing to work to achieve the vision; and the technical ability to carry out the vision" (p. 13). Kotter (1990) tells us that "the direction-setting aspect of leadership does not produce plans; it creates vision and strategies" (p. 104). Potts and Behr (1987) say that "today's more competitive world" requires not just a manager but a leader "who also has the vision to understand what is changing . . . and can adapt quickly to take advantage of that change" (p. 10). Tichy and Ulrich (1984) maintain that the "transformational" leader is one who can "develop and communicate a vision and get others to commit to it" (p. 251).

It appears that the leader's vision provides guidance to the organization—helps it find new directions and chart a successful course in a world beset with complexity. In this respect, contemporary organizational literature simply expands on the ideas of classic writers like Barnard and Selznick. Barnard (1948) argued a half a century ago that "The primary efforts of leaders need to be directed to the maintenance and guidance of organizations as whole systems of activities," a capacity that in turn requires the ability to distinguish "effectively between the important and the unimportant *in the particular concrete situation*" (pp. 89, 86). Selznick (1957), for his part, says that the leader "provides guidance to minimize [organizational] blindness . . . his imagination is stirred by the processes of group interaction and the vision of a harmonious team" (pp. 135, 137).

This emphasis on vision as a characteristic leadership quality is notable because of the centuries-old association between vision and the kind of cognition typically seen as masculine (Keller &

Grontkowski, 1983). In ancient Greece, the transition from an oral to a literate culture—from Homer to Plato—produced a change in the idea of knowledge, from identification and engagement with the concrete to detachment and abstraction. The essence of the change is symbolized by a shift in the site of knowledge acquisition from the ear to the eye. In Plato's work, intellect becomes the "eye of the mind" (Keller & Grontkowski, 1983, p. 210); because of its "apparent incorporeality," vision "promotes the illusion of disengagement and objectification" (p. 213). And while for Plato the idea of knowledge included connection with the truth as well as distance from the world, by the time of Newton the eye had become "the means of establishing a total and radical severance of subject and object" (p. 216). Drawing on the work of Hans Jonas, Keller and Grontkowski suggest that vision persists as a metaphor for knowledge because, of all the senses, it alone offers the illusion of timelessness and thus a basis for objectivity and the hope of eternal truth, which I have already suggested are culturally masculine concerns.

If we extend this reasoning to the connection between vision and leadership, a curious relationship between the leader and other members of the organization (the led) begins to emerge. If the leader is a visionary, then others in the situation become objects of the leader's gaze. Grosz (1990) argues:

> Vision performs a distancing function, leaving the looker unimplicated in or uncontaminated by its object. . . . As Sartre recognized, the look is the domain of domination and mastery; it provides access to its object without necessarily being in contact with it. (p. 38)

Thus vision is not simply a matter of seeing but also of controlling, of fixing and defining those who are the object of the gaze. I do not mean to imply that these "others" necessarily perceive themselves this way. But if the leader's vision is the necessary ingredient in organizational coherence, development, and direction, then without realizing it other organizational members have ceded control to him not only of the organization but of themselves and crucial aspects of their self-definitions. In the brasher treatments of leadership this tendency becomes quite explicit, as when Potts and Behr (1987) laud the ability to "see where a company has to go . . . and [to] chart a course that can get the company to that goal, pulling legions of employees along the way" (p. 200).

Consideration of the leader as decision maker reinforces this perception. In public administration, we have thought of the administrator as a decision maker at least since Woodrow Wilson (1887/1978), who held that "the administrator should have and does have a will of his own in the choice of means for accomplishing his work. He is not and ought not to be a mere passive instrument" (p. 12). Barnard (1948) argued that "the ability to make decisions is the characteristic of leaders I think most to be noted. It depends on a propensity or willingness to decide and a capacity to do so" (p. 94). Today, as Thompson (1985) tells us, "almost all government textbooks refer to political courage as the master virtue in politics, the ability to make decisions" (p. 6). Similarly, books on business management praise decisiveness, the willingness and ability to take charge.[2]

The cultural masculinity of the decision maker is revealed in the work of some of our most influential thinkers. For example, Freud argued that people have a need for authority, which, because of its "decisiveness of thought, . . . strength of will . . . [and] energy of action are part of the picture of a father" (quoted in Kets de Vries, 1989, p. 26). According to Bologh, Weber believed strong political leaders would rescue substantive political ends from being overwhelmed by bureaucratic means, in other words, by sheer process. From Weber's perspective, efficiency also required a strong leader; democratizing organizational decision making would undermine rationality. For Weber, "one either adopts a feminine attitude of passivity in which 'life is permitted to run on as an event in nature' or one adopts a masculine emphasis on decisive action in which life is 'consciously guided by a series of ultimate decisions' " (Bologh, 1990, p. 101).

Feminist organization theorists have also pointed out how decision making and mastery are associated with masculinity. Kanter (1977) argues that in organizations men are rewarded for decisiveness, rationality, and visible leadership and women for routine service; in Kanter's view, men and women in effect constitute separate organizational classes regardless of their individual positions in the hierarchy. Smircich (1985) suggests that the culturally masculine desire to master events and processes shapes and permeates management theory. Theorists of public administration, for their part, invoke gender implicitly. Terry (1990) praises the proactive efforts of administrative "conservators" to preserve institutional integrity while he rejects weakness and subservience on the part of public administrators. Rohr's (1989) examination of the "inherent ambiguity" of executive power turns on the tension between the origin of the word *executive*, which means "follower, or one who carries out" (that is, a clerk) and a more edifying connotation, such as is reflected in the president's executive privilege, in terms of which the executive is "clearly a leader" (p. 108).

Of course the leadership literature does not portray leaders simply as take-charge types pursuing their individual visions come what may. The leader is also one who inspires others, who in Selznick's (1957) words "knows how to transform a neutral body of men into a committed polity" (p. 61). The leader's inspiration is said to motivate subordinates to carry out their work efficiently (Maccoby, 1988), sometimes to do things beyond their normal capabilities (Kets de Vries, 1989). Even more important, the leader entices workers to put the organization's goals (as defined by its leadership) ahead of their own, in return for various inducements (Barnard, 1938)—an arrangement that, in graduate school, I heard described as a *Faustian bargain*.

How does the leader effect this bargain with other organizational members? Partly by persuasion (Barnard, 1948) but also by acting as an exemplar and a symbol of organization purposes. We hear the corporation referred to as "the lengthened shadow of a man" (Doig & Hargrove, 1987, p. 20), but the shadow also extends beyond organizational boundaries. Lewis (1980) notes that "thousands of would-be public and private managerial types now emulate [leaders] consciously and unconsciously, for [they] have become cultural archetypes" (p. 244). One such archetype might be John F. Welch, Jr., chief executive officer of General Electric:

They call him Neutron Jack. . . . In the past five years he has cut a swathe through the huge company, overseeing the closing of more than a score of plants and the idling of thousands of workers. When Neutron Jack hits a GE plant town, they say, the people disappear, but the building still stands. . . .

But Welch is no wild-eyed renegade on an ego trip. . . . His overhaul of GE is bringing [it] up to date . . .making . . . GE competitive and successful in [a] rapidly changing world. (Potts & Behr, 1987, pp. 1-3)

Or the exemplar might be Admiral Arleigh Burke:

> "30-knot Burke," the sailors called him . . . because he always kept his task force moving at flank speed. "This is a guy that sailors would walk off the edge of a cliff for," [Ross] Perot says. "He was not a remote, distant figure. He was a guy down there." (Potts & Behr, 1987, p. 207)

Warrior or father figure, such characters are said to serve as inspirational symbols, spurring the rest of us to extraordinary effort, albeit frequently in aid of goals we have had little part in selecting. That our ability to identify with such figures may vary depending on the content of our own self-images is only imperfectly noted (a point expanded on in chapter 5).

The American government's felt need for inspirational leaders is apparently of long-standing. As Skowronek (1982) notes, "Federalists and Jeffersonians alike hoped for a consensus of enlightened leaders in a government designed to produce conflicts of interest . . . Their successes were precariously dependent on the exceptional man [and] the personal loyalties he could instill in others" (p. 24). Crenson (1975) comments that the Jacksonians inherited this dependence, which they reflected in the informal control executive officers had over their departments: "The personal characteristics and preferences of administrative chieftains carried more weight than formal administrative arrangements" (p. 52). In the Progressive era, Croly (1909/1963) praised the inspirational qualities of Theodore Roosevelt, who "exhibited his genuinely national spirit in nothing so clearly as in his endeavor to give to men of special ability, training, and eminence a better opportunity to serve the public" (p. 170).

Through inspiring organizational members and instilling in them loyalty to the organization and its goals, the leader also shapes their perceptions of the meaning of their work and their lives; in addition to imparting value to rationalized work, the leadership activity that Selznick called *institutionalization* is also a process of reality creation. Writers on leadership argue that, through vision, through ability to sense the terms of the organization's environment and to articulate the organizational mission, the leader "brings order out of chaos. . . . We need someone to look up to or blame. The mere presence of individuals willing to take on the leadership role facilitates the organization of experience and in so doing helps us acquire a sense of control over our environment" (Kets de Vries, 1989, pp. 22-23). As we saw in the previous chapter, the theme of bringing order out of disorder associates the former with the masculine and the latter with the feminine. The sort of symbolic power in question, of course, extends outside the organization. Crenson (1975), for instance, observes that the emotional bond Andrew Jackson established between himself and Americans of the time "told men how they felt" (p. 29). In his study of public entrepreneurs, Lewis (1980) notes that J. Edgar Hoover "controlled and specified the reality premises about crime for the whole society" (p. 119). The ultimate power of the leader, then, is "To make mankind in conscious virtue bold, / Live o'er each scene, and be what they behold" (Alexander Pope, quoted in Wills, 1984, p. 125). The question, however, is what is involved in becoming what we behold: How great a part of our existing identities we must abandon or reshape in the process of emulating leaders, of letting them suggest to us the meaning of our work or the nature of our very selves. While it is certainly not impossible for people who are "different" in race, gender, or socioeconomic status to identify with or be inspired by upper-class white male leaders, the process is a more complex one than for those whose characteristics more closely match those of the typical mainstream model.

WOMEN LEADERS

The characteristics that they criticize you for, that you are strong-minded, that you make firm and tough decisions, are also characteristics which, if you were a man, they would praise you for. I think they have not yet fully come to terms with that.

Margaret Thatcher (quoted in " 'Iron Lady,' " p. A1.)

Women who move into leadership positions in public agencies find themselves presented with a dilemma. The accepted understanding of leadership entails an image that white, professional-managerial men fit rather well and others have difficulty matching. In Western industrialized societies, both men and women expect leaders to be decisive, visionary, bold, and inspirational; as we will see, they also tend to expect leaders to be male. The qualities frequently associated with women, such as intuition and nurturance, are beginning to make their way into discussions of leadership, but are still nowhere near being seen as definitive (Stivers, 1991).

As a result, women who become or aspire to become leaders in public agencies are faced with a complex task of self-definition. If they strive to display the expected characteristics, they risk being seen as masculine (inappropriately so, of course) and depending on their individual personalities may feel a certain amount of dissonance between their sense of themselves as women and what is expected of them as leaders. If, on the other hand, they attempt to embody and reflect a different image of leadership than the conventional one, they risk being viewed as unequal to the leadership role—as indecisive, soft, not assertive enough. Admittedly, some men may also feel dissonance between their personal styles and what is expected of leaders, and a man's failure to meet leadership standards is occasionally chalked up to deficient masculinity (for example, the "wimp factor" that plagued the pre-Willie Horton George Bush). Men, however, are never criticized as women are for being successful leaders; men are never accused of having undergone the equivalent of a sex change by virtue of having assumed a leadership role.

As a result of this dissonance between womanhood and leadership, a number of stereotypes have grown up about women leaders. The *earth mother* brings cookies to meetings; the *pet* serves as work group mascot; the *manipulator* uses feminine wiles to get her way; the *workaholic* does not know how to delegate; the *iron maiden* tries too hard and is seen as tyrannical (a recent biography of Margaret Thatcher is titled *The Iron Lady*); the *egalitarian* denies her own power by claiming to relate to subordinates as colleagues (Heller, 1982, p. 3). Women leaders who escape such labels often have their images rendered acceptable by more subtle means. For example, Wyszomirski's (1987) portrait of Nancy Hanks describes her in these terms: "A single, attractive, middle-aged woman who combined femininity with a sense of traditional propriety, Hanks became one of only a handful of female federal executives, but she was no feminist" (p. 214). Wyszomirski does not define what she means by "feminist," say why she does not consider Hanks a feminist, or specify the basis on which it is undesirable to be one. These images convey something of the "damned if you do, damned if you don't" quality of the juggling act in which women leaders engage. Womanhood per se is problematic in the organizational context. Because the stereotypical characteristics of white professional men such as rationality and task orientation match the defining qualities of bureaucracy, we tend to see such qualities (just as we see the organization itself) as neutral rather than masculine. In the bureaucracy, only women have gender and, therefore, a problem accommodating to the dynamics of organizational life. The leader's masculinity is seen as normal, while the qualities of the women who surround him—for example, female secretaries and clients—represent that which the leader is not (helpful, acquiescent); such women are acceptable because they are subordinate and therefore nonthreatening. In contrast, women in nonclerical positions evoke in the male eye (consciously or unconsciously) the intrusion of the private—the sexual—into the level of public life that men occupy (Hearn & Parkin, 1988). Used to seeing women either as sex objects or as surrogates for their mothers, daughters, or wives, male managers have difficulty seeing them as leaders or peers. Furthermore, as Kanter (1977) argues, women and men constitute separate organizational classes, with women (in general) rewarded for routine service and men for rational decision making and leadership. According to Kanter, the surface similarity between women managers and the largely female clerical staff tends to interfere with women's ability to exercise leadership regardless of their individual management style or competence.

Research indicates that both men and women overwhelmingly expect leaders to be men, so much so that women in jobs that should logically be considered leadership positions—such as the head nurse of a state hospital—have not been generally recognized as such:

A number of studies have shown that stereotypes of how men differ from women match very well our perception and evaluation of how leaders differ from followers. . . . Men, but not women, are characterized as aggressive, independent, objective, active, dominant, competitive, and decisive, whereas traits attributed to women clustered around gentleness, emotionality, sensitivity, dependency, submissiveness. . . . Schein, for example, has demonstrated in several studies that male as well as female managers . . . perceive themselves as possessing and demonstrating characteristics, attitudes, behaviors, and temperaments more commonly ascribed to men than women. (Kruse & Wintermantel, 1986, p. 176)

Astin and Leland (1991) point out that, while studies show no clear pattern of difference in behavior between male and female leaders, subordinates react differently to similar behavior according to whether the leader is a man or a woman. These authors also note that much of the research on the relationship between gender and leadership has been conducted in terms of traditional models such as trait theory, contingency theory, and so on often developed in laboratory or other settings where males predominate.

The lopsided organizational distribution of the sexes, with men occupying all or all but a few of the top positions and women concentrated in low-level clerical and staff support positions, is a structural source of expectations about leadership. There are many factors influencing the discriminatory practices that result in this apportionment, including cultural values that assign men responsibility for public activities and women private ones, and organizational expectations that white-collar men will be *mind* workers and white-collar women, manual workers. In addition, some observers theorize the existence of a dual labor market in which women function as a "reserve army of labor" based on their performance of household and child-care duties (Hearn & Parkin, 1988, p. 18); capitalism's structural necessity for surplus workers supports patterns in which women are disproportionately restricted to low-level, often part-time, organizational positions.

The feedback loop between the sexual distribution of labor and people's expectations about who will occupy what job means that women who aspire to leadership roles encounter material and mental barriers to their access to such positions; when they do manage to move into a leadership position, women face the difficult task of managing their femininity. The management literature reflects no small amount of advice on how to do this, but little if any acknowledgment that it is anything but an individual problem. One line of thought simply accepts the mainstream definition of leadership and advocates the elimination of barriers to women's access to top positions. This approach is characteristic of liberal feminism, which advocates a piece of the existing action for women. The expectation is that as women become leaders and show that they can be tough, bold, and so on, leadership will gradually lose its association with masculinity. In the leadership literature based on this view, the focus is on teaching women to be better at leadership as men have exemplified it, in order for them to qualify for the equal opportunities that revamped hiring and promotion policies are said to open up to them. Themes include fitting in and learning the men's game. These books tell women they are responsible for their own success or failure in adapting to organizational life; their primary task is to adjust their own femaleness. Harragan's (1981) *Games Mother Never Taught You*, for example, advises women to use football jargon and military imagery around the office. *Leadership Skills for Women* counsels "business-like clothing and sensible heels that increase your height . . . strong, direct language. . . . Do not overuse hand gestures. . . . Do not flirt. . . . Don't try to be 'one of the boys' " (Manning, 1989, p. 15).

In recent years, considerable attention has been paid to the possibility that, because women have different personal qualities and life experiences than men, they tend to approach organizational leadership distinctively, and that these differences may benefit organizations, helping them achieve the greater flexibility required in an era of increasing complexity. From this perspective, the task is not to try and wipe out women's feminine qualities but to use them to enhance organizational effectiveness. Women's management styles are said to be less hierarchical and more participatory: "Women value connections and community and sharing power. We want the world to be a family," says management consultant Bev Forbes (quoted in Grubb, 1991, p. 18). Women leaders are reported to try "to make people feel part of the organization . . . encouraging others to have a say in almost every aspect of the work. . . . They create mechanisms that get people to participate and they use a conversational style that sends signals inviting people to get involved" (Rosener, 1990, p. 120).

Helgesen's (1990) case study of four women executives, which examined how they differed from the males studied in Mintzberg's (1973) well-known *The Nature of Managerial Work,* reported that the women departed significantly from Mintzberg's picture of *ordinary* managerial behavior. They were willing to be what Mintzberg called *interrupted* by unscheduled tasks and visits, out of a desire to keep the organizational fabric in good repair; they shared rather than hoarded information; instead of identifying wholly with their careers, they saw themselves as multifaceted. Along similar lines, a *New York Times* profile of Grace Pastiak, director of manufacturing for Tellabs, Inc., described her as preferring a personalized, walking-around approach, trying to imbue her subordinates with the enthusiasm for quality (Holusha, 1991).

The expectation reflected in much of the writing in this vein is that as more women move into leadership positions, organizations themselves will begin to change—will become less hierarchical, more participative, and more humane. Kanter's (1980) position, however, counsels skepticism about this argument. She suggests that whatever differences are perceived between men's and women's organizational behavior are a function of power rather than sex: "Every statement that can be made about what women typically do or feel holds true for some men. . . . What appear to be 'sex differences' in work behavior emerge as responses to structural conditions, to one's place in the organization" (Kanter, 1980, p. 57). Kanter's argument raises two possibilities. One is that feminine management techniques, despite the praise they now seem to be receiving in certain quarters, remain disadvantageous to women overall: They tend to reinforce cultural stereotypes that work against women's equal access to top jobs, and most of the women who employ them ultimately find themselves, with other women, bumping up against the glass ceiling that prevents them from rising to the very top of the organization. The other possibility is that current attention to women's different leadership styles is simply a reflection of greater overall interest in participative management, a tendency away from overtly hierarchical and militaristic management toward strategies such as *total quality management.* One professor of management has noted this as the key management trend of the past 25 years and, as such, a helpful development for women managers (Holusha, 1991). The ultimate effect on organizational structure of this wave of kinder, gentler management has yet to be determined, however. Humane management styles may simply ease the process of getting employees to buy into organizational goals set at the top (Argyris, 1957; Grenier, 1988). In this case, women's feminine leadership is not really in the process of transforming organizations, only of masking their real nature more effectively. Meanwhile the feedback loop between the sexual distribution of labor in organizations and people's expectations about who can do which job remains a barrier to women's advancement into the leadership of public agencies and private corporations. For the foreseeable future, authorities like *Fortune* magazine will continue to tell women who aspire to organizational leadership, "Look like a lady; act like a man; work like a dog" (Fierman, 1990, p. 62).

LEADERSHIP AND PUBLIC ADMINISTRATION

To conclude this chapter, my brief against using our supposed need for public sector leadership to argue for the legitimacy of public administration is that our images of leadership are not only limited to traits many of which are associated with white professional males but result in material disadvantage to those who appear to depart from them. We have a circular situation in which men (almost always white men) occupy the top organizational jobs; we look to current leaders for our ideas about what and who leaders are; these ideas serve as filters, screening out everyone but those who meet the accepted standards; therefore, the leaders remain the same and so do the standards. When those who are different do manage to attain a leadership position, they face a continual struggle to deal with the disparity between what people expect of leaders and what is expected of them because of ascribed characteristics like sex and race. As we saw was the case with the image of expertise, the leadership argument privileges masculine qualities over feminine ones and supports a distribution of labor in which people who are not white professional males are at a disadvantage.

In addition, as chapter 3 concluded with respect to expertise, arguments about the need for public sector leadership and how public administrators fill the bill reflect an effort to deny structural features of public administration that reflect culturally feminine qualities. As Rohr (1986, 1989) points out, members of the executive branch—at least those who exercise any significant amount of administrative discretion—are both leaders and clerks: They carry out orders but they also give them. The legislature, court and chief executive are the masters of public administrators, who are expected to be subservient to them; but "The Public Administration" frequently has the option to choose which master it will obey. Rohr's discussion of this dual nature is more explicit than most about the need for subservience on the part of public administrators; more typically, public administrators are told they must "not be weak or subservient" (Terry, 1990, p. 407). Taking orders is seen as weakness; although awareness of it may not always be conscious, those who prototypically give orders are white males and those who take them women and people of color. When subjected to an analysis on the basis of gender, the image of the public servant remains paradoxical—claimed for its high moral tone, yet resisted due to its silent femininity. If this were not so, we would be discussing various arguments for the legitimacy of public administration based on its faithful obedience to the people, or the motherliness with which it keeps the public's house. In actuality, much of the work of public agencies does *not* involve significant exercise of discretionary power but simply the execution of routine, unglamorous, but generally necessary duties— work much like housework, and like it, undervalued.

Looking through the lens of gender, the entire notion of leadership—and our purported need for it—is subject to question. Rather than accepting the idea that people need someone to look up to or to tell them what to do, some theorists have asked why this appears to be so and suggested that perhaps under other material circumstances leadership might not seem so necessary, or, more accurately, we might see leadership differently. We might see it as a necessary coordinative role that many if not most organizational members are perfectly capable of fulfilling, a position that is occupied by any one member only temporarily. Ferguson (1984) has suggested that perhaps leadership could consist as much (maybe more) in being at the center of a network of relationships as it does in being at the top of a pyramid. Astin and Leland (1991) see leadership as inherently a social change process that puts a premium on the empowerment of others and the creation of networks for joint effort. Because most of us have so little experience with any such arrangements and because business as usual seems so firmly entrenched, most such ideas are dismissed as terribly impractical. I take up this question again in the final chapter. For now, regardless of how practical or impractical alternatives may be, the idea of leadership remains deeply gendered and fundamentally problematic for women. This should be enough to reopen the question of how worthy a basis it is for defending the legitimacy of public administration.

NOTES

1. Travis (1991) presents personal accounts of the difficulties African-American men and women have in being perceived as leaders, let alone competent employees, by their corporate or public agency co-workers.

2. I have observed the same respect for decisiveness in many of my students: In work groups they praise the person who takes charge as task oriented and criticize a process orientation (for example, making sure that all members of the group participate in framing an approach to the task) as a time-wasting diversion from the job at hand.

5

The Hero Factory:
The Dilemma of Virtue

The rectitude of public servants is an enduring concern, not just in the literature of public administration but in the world of government and politics and among the American people at large. Much of what is written and said about the moral status of public administrators is either skeptical or hortatory: Muckrakers, in time-honored fashion, go after the sloth and corruption of bureaucrats (the magazine *Washington Monthly* is a good contemporary example of the genre), while ethicists seek to fashion moral arguments that will inspire worthy administrative behavior. Normative public administration theory, on the other hand, focuses as much on *asserting* the virtue of public administrators as on trying to guide or find fault with it. While defenders of public administration recognize imperfections in the practice of administrative morality, they argue that the essence of public service lies in commitment to the common good and that public administrators are due a certain amount of respect for their willingness to make that commitment. According to this perspective, the legitimacy of administrative authority can be traced to the public-spiritedness of its exercise, which—if only citizens become aware of it—will win their support of their government and thus preserve the polity. This logic echoes Alexander Hamilton's reasoning in *Federalist* 27 that the people's "confidence in and obedience to a government, will commonly be proportioned to the goodness or badness of its administration" (Cooke, 1961, p. 172). While they recognize the shortcomings of public administrators, then, apologists believe it important to emphasize their civic virtue in order to maintain, or win back, "the respect and attachment of the community" (p. 173).

Many of the arguments linking the legitimacy of public administration to the virtue of administrators also echo Hamilton in their view of the people as the ultimate source of governmental authority but in need of protection against their own errors and delusions. As White (1948) pointed out, the Federalists "accepted the philosophy of government for the people, but not government by the people. In their view, government could only be well conducted if it was in the hands of the superior part of mankind—superior in education, in economic standing, and in native ability" (p. 508). Now as then, it seems, discussions of virtue occasionally cross the fine line between asserting the rectitude of public administrators and claiming their moral superiority to the people at large.

Four images of the virtuous public administrator mark the arguments I consider in this chapter: the guardian (or trustee or steward) of regime values, the seeker after fame and honor, the hero, and the citizen. Once again, I will draw attention to the gender dilemmas these images raise, not only because they are culturally masculine but also because they contribute to keeping women at a disadvantage, both in society and within public administration itself. In contrast to the discussions of expertise and leadership, however, the exploration of ideas about virtue in public administration will bring to light the extent to which in American political and social history virtue has been considered a feminine quality. I will suggest that the perceived femininity of virtue has contributed to its continued status as a private rather than civic notion, and that the assertive masculinity marking images of virtue in public administration reflects an attempt, albeit unconscious, to counteract associations with womanly benevolence. As a prelude to analyzing the images themselves, I begin with a brief review of the idea of virtue in the history of American political thought. The chapter concludes with a few reflections on what the gender dilemmas surrounding ideas of virtue appear to imply about the legitimacy of public administration.

VIRTUE

In the arguments under consideration, the administrator's public-spiritedness wins the esteem of citizens and fosters popular virtue. The virtuous public administrator not only protects and upholds the public interest but serves as an exemplar of virtue to others (see Cooper & Wright, 1992) and is qualified to educate the public to greater public spiritedness (Gawthrop, 1984) or to the practice of benevolence (Frederickson & Hart, 1985). The virtue of public administrators is *public* in the sense that they act on behalf of the people and because they do so visibly, if not to the eyes of the people themselves then certainly to those of elected representatives. The public administrator's virtue is strikingly performative. In carrying out their responsibilities, public administrators display the content of their individual characters to all observers and spur some, at least, to nobler aims—virtue "by contagion," Hume called it (Wills, 1984, p. 115).

The idea of virtue that characterizes the contemporary literature is the product of a long developmental process. Over more than 2,000 years, the meaning of the word *virtue* has undergone a number of transformations (Cooper, 1992). For Aristotle, virtue entailed wide-ranging excellences of character, including moral ones, which could be cultivated and which produced a balanced person capable of leading the good (therefore public) life. The character trait emphasis is also found in the four cardinal virtues of the classical period: prudence, justice, temperance, and courage; the Christian era added three theological virtues: faith, hope, and love. During the Enlightenment, Hume made virtue synonymous with obeying laws or moral rules rather than with specific character traits. By the time of the Federalists, a view of human nature as turbulently passionate and in need of control made the idea of virtue as an aspect of character seem undependable, unless it was equated with desire for fame on the part of the better sort (see below); thus the framers of the Constitution perceived the need for a governmental structure that would supply "the defect of better motives," so that "interest would do the work of virtue."

Notions of class also affected the Federalists' understanding of virtue, which in their eyes was linked to the concept of the gentleman. The gentleman of Elizabethan England, an ideal that subsequently reached America, was a man of virtue, learning, and wealth; occasionally theory allowed that wealth was less important than virtue and learning, but in practice the three were inextricably linked, as this observation from John Adams suggests:

> The people, in all nations, are naturally divided into two sorts, the gentlemen and the simplemen. . . . By gentlemen are not meant the rich or the poor, the high-born or the low-born, the industrious or the idle; but all those who have received a liberal education. . . . We must nevertheless remember that *generally* those who are rich, and descended from families in public life, will have the best education in arts and sciences, and therefore the gentleman will ordinarily be the richer, and born of more notable families. (quoted in White, 1948, p. 548)

The current interest in virtue on the part of public administration scholars represents a return to a fuller understanding than the one that moved the framers; it includes a developmental view of humanity and a set of positive qualities instead of a fixed notion of human nature that relies heavily on adherence to laws or rules. The modern version is intended to be open to all human beings and not just well-educated males of good family. Within this renewal of the idea of virtue, however, is an unexamined assumption. The virtue under discussion—good citizenship, or willingness to put the common good ahead of personal interests—is *public* virtue. Because Western culture since ancient Greece has associated the public with men and the private with women, an association that barred women from public life for more than two millenia, the idea of public virtue as a model for public administration deserves a bit more scrutiny.

According to Bloch (1987), the idea of public virtue in the Revolutionary period drew on both classical republican and Protestant traditions. Within classical republicanism, virtue was a public quality fostered in a society characterized by property holding and mixed government; the virtue of the propertied was expressed in their participation in ruling, while that of the people at large showed itself in popular rising against invasion or corruption and in loyalty to the regime. Within Protestantism, virtue came from faith, and was mainly a trait of good rulers, while other members of the community simply obeyed their rules and lived according to moral strictures. Both traditions, however, agreed that public virtue was masculine, while the private, Christian virtues were seen as equally accessible to both sexes. The masculinity of the republican version was particularly pronounced, derived as it was from the Homeric idea of excellence tied to physical courage in battle, and from Greek and Roman notions about cooperative endeavor among male citizens of the state. The masculinity of virtue is visible in Machiavelli's republican thinking: By taking political action, men achieve mastery over circumstances—that is, they outwit *fortuna*, a woman (Pitkin, 1984). Such understandings were reinforced throughout much of Western history by laws that barred women from public life; thus their significance is not just attitudinal.

During the 1780s and 1790s, according to Bloch (1987), a uniquely feminine understanding of public spiritedness began to emerge. According to the terms of *republican motherhood*, women could partake of public virtue by encouraging it in their husbands and fostering it in their sons (see also Kerber, 1980). This ideology fixed the wellspring of virtue in the home rather than in the public space itself; therefore, it supported a political shift away from reliance on the efforts of free men participating together and toward the establishment of a constitutional order that put little weight on such participation, in fact, restricted it. This shift "made it possible to preserve the notion of public virtue while at the same time divesting it of its former constitutional significance" (Bloch, 1987, p. 56). Thus, whether consciously or not, the idea of home as the source of virtue supported the Federalists' position: Letting "interest do the work of virtue" in public became acceptable because virtue could be seen as doing its work in the private sphere. The purpose of the Constitution was to protect private virtues (as well as individual liberty), not to promote public ones. Virtue became "ever more difficult to distinguish from private benevolence, personal manners, and female sexual propriety" (Bloch, 1987,

p. 56). In practical terms, what public virtue remained consisted only of voting and a vague allegiance to the idea of the country, as it became symbolized in the flag and celebrated on public holidays. The confinement of virtue to domestic and social activities increasingly made it seem feminine and blurred the moral distinction between men's political activities and their self-interested economic pursuits. It became more and more difficult to expect (or at least to assume) that political behavior was driven by public spiritedness rather than the hope of individual gain.[1] Masculinity became associated less with living the good public life than with the rational pursuit of self-interest, whether in business or in government, an association that contributed to the perception of self-interest as an inevitable or natural aspect of society outside the home. During the 19th century (as the next chapter sets forth in detail), the femininity associated with ideas of virtue persisted, reinforced by cultural distinctions drawn between two modes of public life—the ostensibly masculine world of party politics and women's "private" charitable work, aimed particularly at helping families in need.

The entrance of women into the fullness of American political life beginning in 1920, and their subsequent infiltration into elected office and into public bureaucracy has reduced neither the sharp distinction still made between public life and the domestic world of home and family nor women's disparate responsibility for the latter. Thus the current attempt in public administration at resuscitation of a substantive interpretation of public virtue is a matter of going against what is still the prevailing flow. Not only must such a project combat the reigning idea that all political activity is self-interested but it must face the persistent commonsense construction of virtue as feminine. Since the days of republican motherhood, virtue in America has been largely associated with private behavior. It is a quality fostered in (and largely confined to) women's sphere, one that typically has to do with female sexual, maternal, or charitable behavior and is therefore seen as weak in comparison to the tough-mindedness and realism expected of public figures. Rhetoric about heroes and guardians notwithstanding, it appears that it will be difficult either to legitimate public administration on the basis of its virtue or to foster virtue in public administrators (or other public figures) as long as people consciously or unconsciously equate virtue with femininity and as long as they fear being seen as feminine—a fear shared by both men and women involved in public life. Founder John Adams once observed, "The people are Clarissa"—that is, the people's virtue is passive and feminine, "destined to be deceived and violated by unscrupulous men in power" (quoted in Bloch, 1987, p. 57). We are in need of an understanding of virtue that is strong without being muscular, active without being competitive, laudable without elitism, selfless without passivity—given the gender dilemmas in our current notions of virtue, a tall order indeed. The following sections explore these dilemmas.

THE GUARDIAN

Many defenders of public administration invoke the idea of the guardian, trustee or steward of public values. We encountered this idea in connection with the notion of professional autonomy (chapter 3). There it was reflected in the Blacksburg perspective (Wamsley et al., 1990), which sees the public administrator as a trustee of the public interest and the public agency as a repository of time-tested wisdom; in Kass's (1990) steward, working on behalf of others; and in Terry's (1990) conservator of administrative capacity. In considering the virtue of public administrators, the aspect of these images on which we want to focus shifts from the autonomy they confer to their moral status as *protector*. Morgan and Kass (1991) summarize this argument:

> The stewardship model contends that the public administrator's highest duty is to protect and nurture the constitutional system of the republic and the constitutive values which the system is meant to realize. The justification for performing this role rests on two considerations that, taken together, seek both to legitimate and limit the exercise of discretionary authority by nonelected career officials. First, administrative agents take an oath to uphold our constitutional order. Second, administrative bodies possess a unique capacity to carry out this oath in a manner that furthers constitutional values. (pp. 45-46)

Here Morgan and Kass suggest that, as a result of having taken an oath of office, public administrators are *more actively committed* to the public interest than the general public, and that they and their agencies are *better qualified* to decide in particular circumstances how to translate constitutional values into specific actions. Frederickson and Hart also see the public administrator as a protector. They "define the primary moral obligation of the public service in this nation as the patriotism of benevolence"; they equate this with protection of "all the people within our political boundaries . . . in all of the basic rights granted to them by the enabling documents" (Frederickson & Hart, 1985, p. 549). These arguments see public administrators as guardians of the individual rights of members of the polity and of the constitutional order itself.

The elitism of the idea of guardianship—always possible, sometimes actual—has been pointed out (for a recent example, see Fox and Cochran, 1990). Yet the idea persists that citizens are in need of protection not only from the depredations of those who would deprive them of their rights but also from the results of their own ignorance, selfishness, and irrationality. From this perspective, the people are not only the vulnerable Clarissa but also the head-strong Emma, in need of chastening, or the shrewish Kate, in need of taming. It is difficult to appeal to the idea of guardianship without at the same time calling forth an attendant cluster of images that render those being guarded either helpless or danger-ous. The protectors of rights can too easily become protectors against the efforts of the possessors of rights to protect them-selves. The people are asked to trust trustees who do not trust them. The age-old question—Who will guard the guardians?—is relevant here. To those outside the system of government, the checks, balances, separated powers and other restraints on administrative power pale beside their own sense of vulnerability to it.

The gender dilemma in the guardian image should be apparent to readers who have come this far in my argument. The public space is a male preserve and the work of statesmanship a mascu-line effort to tame *fortuna* and control the archetypically feminine, unruly people. Guardians are paternal figures—heads of the pub-lic household—who tell other members, perhaps gently but cer-tainly firmly, what is best for them. The public spiritedness of the protected people, like the virtue of women, lies in obedience and loyalty. The significance of the guardian image is as an effort to instill masculinity in the idea of virtue, to make it strong by making it fatherly. I should note that Morgan and Kass's (1991) analysis contains within it the potential for a less paternal rendering of the guardian, in their reference to the protector as nurturer and to public administrators as "midwives of change." I explore these ideas in the last chapter. For now, it is enough to note that the masculinity of the guardian image—the first of our four modes of virtue—makes it a problem for women in the administrative state; long-standing expectations about the private nature of women's proper role and sphere are inconsistent with the image of public guardian.

THE SEEKER AFTER FAME AND HONOR

I'm Nobody! Who are you?
Are you—Nobody—Too?
Then there's a pair of us?
Don't tell! they'd advertise—you know!

How dreary—to be—Somebody!
How public—like a Frog—
To tell one's name—the livelong June—
To an admiring bog!

Emily Dickinson (in T. Johnson, 1960, p. 133)

The framers of the Constitution envisaged a system in which the work of government would be carried on by the better sort—by virtuous and educated gentlemen. They did not expect all such men to be naturally attracted to the burdens of public office; in fact, they knew that such responsibilities were at best a mixed blessing. In 1816, John Adams advised a young friend:

You must steel your heart and prepare your mind to encounter multitudes of political enemies, and to endure all the buffetings without which there is no rising to distinction in the American world. When the knaves and fools open upon you in full pack, take little or no notice of them, and be careful not to lose your temper. Preserve your private character and reputation unsullied, and confine your speculations upon public concerns to objects of high and national importance. (quoted in White, 1951, pp. 197-198 n.)

What the founders believed would induce men of talent and character to endure the difficulties of governing the republic was the desire for fame and honor, which they considered a noble motive. It was an idea with a long history: In the Roman era, for example, Cicero observed that "public esteem is the nurse of the arts and all men are fired to application by fame" (quoted in Braudy, 1986, p. 56). But at the time of the founding, the passion for fame and honor had a special meaning. According to Adair's (1974) account, the desire for fame involved acting "before an audience of the wise and the good"; it is "a noble passion because it can transform ambition and self-interest into dedicated effort for the community" (p. 11)—thus it harmonizes with the framers' intent to let interest do the work of virtue. The related desire for honor, Adair tells us, while also worthy is somewhat less noble because its connotation of "dignity appropriate to . . . station" (p. 11) makes it inherently exclusive; the Virginia gentleman's code of honor, Adair argues, was able to encompass chattel slavery and treatment of women as intellectual inferiors. For Adair, the passion for fame is particularly commendable because of its public character; essentially it is the desire of "a man to make history, to leave the mark of his deeds and his ideals on the world" (p. 11). Mainzer (1964), on the other hand, sees honor as a mixture of "inner quality and public judgment" that has a "peculiarly social basis" because "the standards for determining honor are communal" (p. 71). But he also finds honor flawed in its class bias and observes that "for women it has been largely confined to chastity—virginity before marriage, fidelity thereafter" (p. 72).

Green (1988) has suggested that modern public administrators, as "prudent constitutionalists," are—and should be—motivated by the desire for fame and honor. Green argues that those who "love the fame of laudable actions" can be entrusted with "great powers" over long periods of time because "their most passionate interests connect with their virtue, and coincide with the duties of office." The result is "a level of insularity sufficient to instill a sense of ownership in the duties of office, and a degree of detachment necessary for exercising wise judgment" (p. 38). Without large powers, which are the prerequisite for attracting an audience of the wise and for leaving one's mark on history, the public administrator may become irresponsible. Linked to power is the prudent constitutionalist's "fair and virtuous independence": even though public administrators—even department heads—are subordinates, their devotion to regime values and to the public good in general legitimates a measure of autonomy appropriate to their role as policymakers. Green contrasts this subordinate independence with what he sees as current stress on a combination of neutral competence and blind loyalty to the political leader. Finally, administrators with due regard for fame and reputation

> will invest a great deal of themselves in their work. They will seek sufficient time and power to realize their plans and policies. In our regime, this requires a great deal of cooperation among the separate powers. Sustained cooperation rests ultimately on the maintenance of "moral understandings or gentlemen's agreements." (Green, 1988, p. 44. Material in quotation marks from Louis Fisher.)

Green concludes that administrators who are willing to make the necessary investment of time and energy in their work will, indeed, "leave the imprint of their character" on their duties (p. 45).

Green's image of the prudent constitutionalist echoes and builds on Alexander Hamilton's ideas about what it would take to make the new government work—in particular, Hamilton's theory that sound administration, by which Hamilton meant administration with real clout, would win the hearts and minds of the people away from excessive attachment to the rival state governments. Sound administration would require men of the better sort, attracted to public service by the prospect of winning public fame. Studies of Hamilton (Adair, 1974; Caldwell, 1988) confirm Green's (1988) assessment of Hamilton as "one of our greatest public administrators" (p. 25). They also portray Hamilton as exceedingly concerned about acquiring fame and leaving his own mark on history. For example, Caldwell (1988) notes: "Tinctured with vanity and a romantic urge to fame, [Hamilton's] purpose was to do some work of truly historic significance" (p. 3). He observes that Hamilton argued for a single head of each department on the basis that "men of the first pretensions will not so readily engage in [boards], because they will be less conspicuous, of less importance, have less opportunity of distinguishing themselves" (p. 45).

Because his ambition was coupled with one of the best analytical minds of his age, Hamilton's life was marked by accomplishments of a scale that ensured that his dream of leaving his imprint on history came true. Before adopting Hamilton as an exemplary image for virtuous public administration, however, perhaps we should explore the gender dilemmas in the Hamiltonian image of the public administrator as seeker after fame and honor. We might begin by noting the nature of Hamilton's *own* exemplars. Adair (1974) points out that, when selecting pseudonyms for certain of his political pamphlets (a common practice at the time), Hamilton picked men of heroic virtue from Greek and Roman history (Phocion, Tully, Camillus, Pericles) who shared "a profound contempt for the people whom they rule and serve so devotedly"; moreover all four "in their biographies are seen to be misjudged, betrayed, persecuted by the miserable populace whose safety and well-being depend on the superman's abilities and services to the state" (pp. 276-278). Hamilton's principal hero, Adair observes, was Julius Caesar, whom he knew through reading Plutarch:

> Plutarch's Caesar is the hero of the world's most sinister success story—a man of transcendent genius who could find self-fulfillment only in the exercise of unchecked power over his fellows. . . . His "love of honor and passion for distinction" led him to court dangers in battle from which his rank would have normally exempted him. Conscious of his genius and certain of what he most desired, he recognized in the social instability and political disorders of Rome the typical revolutionary circumstances which could be exploited in his own pursuit of power, a power which would be used to restore social order and gain him immortal fame. (p. 279)

Finding a number of striking parallels between Julius Caesar's career and Hamilton's own, Adair concludes that Hamilton secretly aimed to succeed George Washington, an ambition that warped his judgment on certain issues and might have led him to "attempt the short and easy way of usurpation of power outside the constitution" if the right circumstances had presented themselves. Acknowledging the need for further research into Hamilton, Adair comments: "No matter how tentatively we say it, until more evidence comes to light, Hamilton would appear to be a statesman who could thus be described in neoclassical rhetoric: 'Curse on his virtues; they have *almost* undone his country' " (p. 284). Looking through the lens of gender, what are we to make of the Hamiltonian public administrator, the seeker after fame, honor, and reputation, the maker of a mark on history, the actor before an audience of the wise and the good? We have already seen that even nonfeminist scholars note the cultural masculinity of the notions of fame and honor. Mainzer (1964) observes that the concept of honor is generally inapplicable to women and criticizes its excessive "brutality," which he says leads us to ignore the gentler aspects of our natures. Adair (1974) notes that the Virginia gentlemen's code of honor did not keep them from owning slaves or from looking on women as intellectual inferiors.

In addition, we encountered in previous chapters certain other difficulties connected with fame and honor. For example, the masculine concern for detachment and independence that I discussed in connection with the interest in autonomy, both for the professional administrator and the administrator as leader, is evidenced here as well. Lerner (1986) notes that "The very concept of honor, for men, embodies autonomy, the power to . . . decide for oneself," a power that even privileged white women, let alone poor women or women of color, have rarely had under patriarchal rule, where they have generally been restricted to the home and their bodies have been at the disposal of their husbands and fathers—or owners and masters (p. 80).[2]

To make one's mark, to be noticed by the wise and good audience, requires independence; one's accomplishments must not disappear into the work of the agency but be singled out for approbation. As we saw in chapter 3, the masculine desire for autonomy is in tension with the feminine expectation of responsiveness. Green (1988) argues, as did Hamilton (and Woodrow Wilson, for that matter), that administrators are both independent and subordinate and that "large powers" promote rather than impede responsibility because of the Hamiltonian administrator's desire for visibility. Green's is a rather paternal if not Olympian notion of responsibility, however, one that includes winning the people's loyalty by protecting them against their own impulses and delusions, thus one that deals with the need for feminine responsiveness by projecting it outward in order to retain the desired independence. Mainzer (1964) notes that personal responsibility and critical ethical thinking are necessary if honor is to be a moral notion:

> For independent, vital expression one must be outside or on top, not a subordinate. . . . If day after day, over years, one is treated as a subordinate in one of the most important functions of his life, this may affect whatever is most basic and continuing about a person. . . . Bettelheim found that to survive as a man, though degraded, in the concentration camps, it was necessary to remain aware of the point beyond which a man would never give in, whatever the price, and to remain aware of one's attitudes toward and reasons for compliance. (pp. 86-88)

Mainzer means to draw attention here to the difficulty of construing bureaucratic behavior as morally responsible. As a woman, however, one cannot read such a passage without reflecting on all the women who have spent their lives, not "outside or on top," but inside or on the bottom, treated as subordinates in every aspect of their lives, and told that their status was worthy (but only for them). Of course, Mainzer has a point: Few *men* have actually spent much time on top of their organizations, but manhood per se has never disqualified them from trying.

We have also encountered (in the discussion of the profession as a brotherhood) Green's idea that Hamiltonian administrators must invest themselves heavily in their work; that discussion pointed out the difficulty for most women in making this sort of investment—how their responsibilities for home life and child rearing tend to preclude their having the same freedom that men do to throw themselves head over heels into their careers. Thus the Hamiltonian image must be problematic for women because of its paternalism and for its basis in a totality of commitment to work that many if not most women find it hard to achieve.

There are a number of additional issues to be raised. One is the psychological assumptions on which the Hamiltonian image is premised. The view of human nature that Hamilton (and most other Federalists) espoused includes the presumption of self-interest coupled with personal ambition. Clearly the supposition that self-interest is the wellspring of virtually all human action is challenged by ideas of maternal love and wifely responsibility for the household; something other than self-interest must lie behind women's willingness to devote so much of their lives to their husbands and children—a willingness on which is predicated the entire liberalist division of life into public and domestic spheres. Personal ambition, too, while not as universalized an assumption as self-interest, ill suits ordinary notions of what animates the lives of women. As we saw was true of the idea of leadership, on a commonsense level ambition is associated with masculinity. In addition, some recent research suggests that women tend not to be driven by the need for external recognition. For example, Markus (1987) found that the women she studied equated achievement with the accomplishment of specific objectives and saw success in private terms such as gaining self-confidence, obtaining credentials under tough circumstances, or coping with their double roles. Markus suggests that only by changing the dominant definition of success (that is, recognition achieved through the single-minded pursuit of a full-time career) will women be able to "succeed" (we would add, and to gain fame and honor). She notes:

> Such a change would mean . . . that women would be able to cease being the "sole repository for repressed human values," that is, they would be able not only to overcome the limitations of the socially ascribed "gender role," but also to bring into public life those behavioral and emotional patterns that are exclusively ascribed to them but which are [now] applicable only in the private sphere. (Markus, 1987, p. 107)

She cautions, however (quoting Ellen Goodman), "It is easier to dress for success than to change the meaning of success" (p. 107).[3]

The publicness of the idea of fame is also problematic, because like every other aspect of the Western idea of the public sphere, it is predicated on the existence of a domestic sphere to which lowly concerns like food, shelter, clothing, and reproduction of the species are consigned along with the women responsible for them. To be in the public sphere is to act before an audience, to see and be seen, an idea that dates back to ancient Greece. Braudy (1986) notes that "in such a theatrical conception of life, when seeing someone from the outside constitutes the most accurate and authentic perspective, the offstage is the obscene" (p. 38).

The desire to make one's distinctive mark on history is also part of the publicness of the quest for fame; in essence this represents a longing for immortality. The activities that form the quest are themselves a rejection of bodily concerns in favor of more lofty issues—that is, those of the mind: in public administrative terms, a repudiation of ministerial and managerial considerations in favor of policymaking and the exercise of discretionary authority. The hoped-for result of these efforts, however—to go down in history and therefore to cheat death— represents the ultimate triumph over the body. Brown's (1988) study finds this theme running through the course of Western political thought, beginning in ancient Greece. She notes that the Greeks both disdained and glorified the body. On the one hand, they praised those bodies that appeared to surpass human limits of beauty or physical prowess. But they equated the ordinary body with animality and—because women seemed to them to be particularly entrapped in their bodies—with femininity; women were therefore seen as threats to men's human freedom and potentiality. Brown observes:

> The Platonic dualism of "being" vs. "becoming" . . . reveals Greek man's conception of the threat posed to his freedom by nature and by the nature he ascribed to women. In politics and philosophy, man strives toward Being (a state occupied by the gods and all immortals) and to escape the mire of Becoming. Becoming is a condition Socrates describes as a "barbaric bog." . . . Becoming, Nature, and Woman are . . . linked to one another and appear to stand for danger and subversion in the mind of Greek man. His fear of *falling into* this barbaric bog was addressed through heroic political and military feats and through zealous pursuit of rational truth. The fear of *being pulled into* this state was dealt with by casting nature and necessity as contaminating, as matter in need of form, and above all, as subject to man's mastery. (pp. 56-57)

Brown argues that the quest to "rise above" the body is politically pernicious because it is used to support policies in aid of a national interest said to require the sacrifice of domestic concerns (those dearest to the hearts of women because of their life experiences), frequently even the literal sacrifice of lives. A secondary result, of course, is that through the equation of women with lesser bodily concerns—those over which the national interest takes precedence—a woman's quest for fame and immortality is fraught with the same tensions as we saw in the cases of professionalism and leadership. Culturally and ideologically, women represent the "barbaric bog"—or perhaps, according to the epigraph at the head of this section, Emily Dickinson's "admiring bog"—while men are the seekers after pure Being (Dickinson's "public frogs"). Stereotypically, women have spent their lives saying "I'm nobody! Who are you?" and taking vicarious pleasure in the accomplishments of their husbands and sons. In actuality, only a relatively small proportion of women have husbands and sons with a real chance at fame and honor, but the force of the stereotype is more widely felt, and blocks the efforts of many different women to identify with this image and to be identified with it by others. In its stress on autonomy, detachment, and independence; in its assumptions of self-interest and ambition; in its publicness and its orientation toward disembodiedness—the image of the Hamiltonian administrator is fraught with gender dilemmas.

THE HERO

A central part of the legitimation effort among public administration theorists in recent years has been the presentation of exemplary figures: real public administrators, living or dead, who embody what is most praiseworthy about public service. One objective of this effort is to show the public at large how laudable the practice of public administration can be; another is to raise the spirits and spur the efforts of civil servants themselves, who have borne the brunt of particularly heavy criticism from all quarters (including presidential) over the last two decades. The idea behind recounting the lives of exemplars is that contemplation of the lives of people struggling toward moral excellence in familiar circumstances engages the emotions and makes us want to strive toward virtue in a way that analysis and the formulation of codes of ethics cannot (Cooper & Wright, 1992).

Recently, Bellavita (1991) has put a different twist on the exemplar, arguing for the notion of the public administrator as hero. Bellavita questioned a group of midlevel bureaucrats about their "personal best organizational experiences." He found that the ways in which administrators characterized their experiences conformed to what Joseph Campbell called the *hero's journey,* a story that takes the form of call to adventure, ordeal, and return. Bellavita uses the framework of the hero's journey to present the stories of several practitioners, with the aim of offering guidance to other public administrators.

Bellavita (1991) suggests that a public administrator undertakes the hero's journey out of a sense of duty, the opportunity to "test an idea or act on a belief" (p. 160) and "the drive to achieve something tangible and meaningful" (p. 161). While the administrative hero, like Campbell's archetype, "has helpers along the way, the journey is fundamentally an individual and voluntary undertaking" (p. 162). The moral import of the hero is found in the willingness to sacrifice "some part of the self for an ideal that is bigger than self. The sacrifice may be time, friendships, reputation, family, career, or on rare occasions life" (p. 174).

As was the case with the guardian and the seeker after fame and honor, the image of the public administrator as hero is a dubious one for women. Terry (1991) has already criticized the hero idea; he asks whether public administration is "so hungry for positive images . . . that we devour them whole" (p. 2) and points to the negative aspects of the hero as the image has come down to us from Homeric times—the hero's violence and recklessness, self-centeredness, stubbornness, and symbolism of male dominance. Although Bellavita does suggest that the hero image is applicable to both men and women, his optimism on this point is belied by the structural masculinity of the hero concept in ancient times, when it took the form in which it has come down to us. Finley (1965) states that " 'hero' has no feminine gender in the age of heroes" (p. 25). He points out that the hero's code, based on physical prowess and honor, admitted no rational discussion of alternatives and included no social obligations—in fact, "the community could grow only by taming the hero and blunting the free exercise of his prowess" (p. 125). In the hero's world

> the inferior status of women was neither concealed nor idealized. . . . In fact, from Homer to the end of Greek literature there were no ordinary words with the specific meanings "husband" and "wife." A man was a man, a father, a warrior, a nobleman, a chieftain, a king, a hero; linguistically, he was almost never a husband. (Finley, 1965, p. 136)

Finley notes that wives were ordinarily referred to as "bedmates."

The question then, as Terry suggests, is whether we can take only the positive aspects of the idea and cast aside the negative ones. Certainly to advocate that we do so implies that our use of symbols and images is driven by conscious rationality, a proposition that I think Campbell himself, as a Jungian, would have rejected. In addition, one's own self-identity affects the ease with which it is possible to pick and choose aspects of images, or to judge certain features as marginal to their impact or relatively unimportant to our assessment of overall moral worth. As an example, consider Blum's (1988) treatment of Oskar Schindler, made famous by Thomas Keneally's *Schindler's List* as a man who, at great personal risk, saved thousands of Jews during World War II. Blum is prepared to judge Schindler a "moral hero" despite his having been a "libertine" and a man with two mistresses in addition to a wife. Blum argues that to disqualify Schindler on the basis of his sexual exploits would constitute a "denial of sensuality and sexuality . . . difficult to justify in terms of the broader perspective of concern for human well-being" (p. 200). Blum suggests that since sexual activity is necessary for physical and emotional health, we must find it difficult to fault Schindler for infidelity. Blum says that, even though it apparently "pained" his wife, Schindler's extramarital activities do not eliminate him out of hand; we would "have to know more about the specific nature" of their relationship. Blum comments: "There is no suggestion that Oskar mistreated Emelie" (p. 200). Blum neglects to tell us what we would have to know about the Schindlers' marriage to make Oskar's infidelity morally acceptable despite the fact that it pained his wife; evidently Blum does not consider the behavior that caused this pain mistreatment. Blum concludes that Schindler's sexual behavior makes him "less of a moral paragon than he would otherwise be; but he remains, I think, a moral hero."

The assessment of Schindler seems to me, however, a more perplexing project than Blum makes it. Blum's (1988) assessment appears to be based on the assumption that sexual transgressions—for example, the breaking of a trust between husband and wife—are less important to a person's overall moral worth than willingness to risk one's life to save the lives of others. Perhaps he is right—but is the one *so* much less significant than the other that we are safe in calling such a man a moral hero? Part of my reluctance to discount Schindler's sexual behavior comes from a sense that the dividing line between public and domestic realms has had the effect of rendering men's domination and mistreatment of women relatively marginal to the assessment of their characters; it may be that, as the historical targets of such behavior, the judgments of women in such cases may take a different shape than men's. Anita Hill's accusation of sexual harassment against Supreme Court nominee Clarence Thomas raised the same question—not only whether Thomas did what Hill said he did, but, if he did, whether these were transgressions important enough to disqualify him. The Senate's failure to conduct a public examination of the issue until after it was leaked to the press suggests that the all-male Judiciary Committee was not troubled enough by this sort of charge to assign it real moral significance. A similar problem confronts us in assessing the moral worth of slave-owning founding fathers; perhaps African-Americans' assessment of the framers' compromise (the legality of slavery in exchange for the southern states' entry into the union) should carry extraordinary moral weight because their ancestors and they have borne the burden of that compromise's "externalities" (see Bell, 1987, for such an assessment).

Examining the notion of hero or exemplar through the lens of gender suggests the need to rework it entirely. First of all, we would want greater consciousness of what our choice of heroes reveals about what is important to us; many heroes in United States culture are quite literally "commanding" figures or those who succeed in intensely competitive efforts—for example, generals ("Stormin' Norman"), professional sportsmen, and business "miracle workers" (Lee Iaccoca). The cultural masculinity of the hero image makes the female hero an anomaly, a challenge to thinking as usual (note that, protopypically, the *heroine* is less the doer of great deeds than the one rescued by the hero). Edwards (1984) suggests that defining heroism in terms of physical strength or social power excludes women, but that coming to see women as heroes can reshape our understanding:

> The woman hero uncovers fractures in the surface of reality. . . . Insofar as she resembles the male hero, she questions the conventional associations of gender and behavior. If . . . she can do as he has done, then patriarchy's prohibitions are a lie. . . . And when she differs

from the male hero, she denies the link between heroism and *either* gender *or* behavior. (pp. 4-5)

Warner's (1981) study of Joan of Arc presents a good example of how a woman hero "fractures . . . the surface of reality." Warner argues that, because in Joan's culture male virtue meant courage while women's meant meekness, she needed a "framework of virtue" that would allow her to "marry her self-image to her actions" (p. 147); therefore, she put on armor, which both protected her against men and "attached men by aping their appearance in order to usurp their functions" (p. 155). Warner points out, however, that Joan never pretended to be a man, and the image of the young girl wearing male armor constituted a symbol that partakes of "a third order" (p. 145)—neither male nor female, but embodying something of both without eclipsing either. Joan thus accomplished what Edwards (1984) suggests the woman hero does: She "upset the tyranny of social fact and revealed its contingency" (p. 237)—leaving in place, however (as Warner notes), "masculinity as the touchstone and equality a process of imitation" (p. 155).

Warner (1981) raises the key question for a gender-based reflection on the hero or exemplar: Can we have images that do not require women to "put on masculinity" in order to qualify? As I have argued elsewhere, so few women have reached positions of significant authority and power in American public life (that is, positions where they come into the public eye) that women aspiring to morally significant lives in the public sector really have little idea what—or whom—they might become (Stivers, 1992a). There is great need to examine the lives of the few women exemplars we do have from a perspective that, instead of unthinkingly measuring them against accepted standards drawn out of contemplating men's lives, reveals their struggle to accomplish without imitating men, their need (as we saw in the discussion on leadership) to manage their femaleness, and the difficulty they have in living according to values and standards many of which the world in which they practice does not share. As we learn more about such women, it may be—as Edwards suggests—that our accepted notions of what constitutes a hero or exemplar will change.

For women in the public sector to serve as exemplars of virtue, we will have to make at least one important structural change in the way we define virtuous lives. We will have to lower the barrier between public and domestic life. This is admittedly a thorny issue; the terms of American political life lead us to treat discussion of private behavior as fit material only for the front pages of tabloids and opportunistic talk-show hosts. Those who long for a return to consideration of substantive issues in political debate see the obsession with the sexual pecadillos of candidates for office as a degradation of electoral politics. Yet the rule that the private lives of public figures should be off limits has costs as well as benefits—making it difficult, for example, in accounts of exemplary lives to deal with moral dilemmas raised by conflicts between public and private obligations. Are people heroes whose single-minded devotion to the public good makes them strangers to their children? Do infidelity or sexual harassment really *count* in our assessment of the worth of public lives? We cannot consider such questions adequately as long as we segregate moral issues into public and private.

We can take this discussion one additional step, however, to ask the question of whether we need exemplars at all. Fisher (1988) argues that models or heroes perpetuate "the logic of domination, by encouraging us to look *up* to 'special women' rather than to look around us for the women with whom we might act" (p. 212). She observes that many women today are striving to lead lives that have no clear precedent because they break with the social roles assigned to women throughout the ages; therefore, exemplars can provide no definitive answers to the dilemmas such women face. Under such conditions, Fisher suggests, creating role models or exemplars is an act of "moral faith," a discovery process, an exploration; but "we find ourselves on a constant moral frontier in which neither our nor anyone else's experience or knowledge of the world guarantees our transition from the present to the future" (p. 217). She concludes:

> Ideal versions of other women's lives can help us in [the] search [for meaning,] but, in the end, the ways in which we present *our own* lives in talking and working with each other have an even greater impact on its outcome . . . not only our successes . . . but also the conditions that have made [them] possible and the contradictions we have failed to overcome. (Fisher, 1988, p. 231; italics added)

From this perspective, we would find our exemplars not by looking up but by looking across, by listening, and by revealing ourselves to one another. We invent the future not by contemplating the marble statues of the founders that came out of 18th-century sculptor Houdon's "hero factory" (Wills, 1984) but by listening to one another's stories and working together.

THE CITIZEN

A fourth image of the virtuous administrator is that of citizen. The major proponent is Cooper (1991, 1984a, 1984b); he argues that "the democratic legitimacy of public administration grows out of the fiduciary nature of the public administrative role. The public administrator is most fundamentally a citizen who acts on behalf of the citizenry in carrying out certain public functions" (1991, p. 4). For Cooper, the ethical obligations of the public administrator are like those of the democratic citizen; they include the practice of horizontal authority relations (power with instead of power over), a search for the public interest, a responsive form of professionalism that wields expertise under the people's sovereignty, and a continuing covenant or set of shared expectations with fellow citizens. Cooper believes that the administrator's most fundamental obligation is to preserve the practice of citizenship itself; duties like maintaining specific institutions and implementing programs are secondary. Acting as a "citizen for the rest of us," Cooper's (1991) citizen-administrator exercises authority on behalf of other citizens and becomes a "witness for the common good," calling on the community itself to become better (p. 161).

Because the energy in Cooper's conceptualization runs horizontally instead of vertically and because he emphasizes the characteristics and values that administrators and other citizens share rather than the things that set them apart, his theory is more appealing than many images of public administration. I return to these aspects of Cooper's argument in my final chapter. Here I want to note one dilemma. Cooper's definition of virtuous citizenship (that which it is the citizen-administrator's ultimate duty to preserve and foster) is "self-interest rightly understood," an idea derived from Alexis de Toqueville. Cooper's enthusiasm for this way of understanding citizenship stems, he says, from a desire to avoid the classical republican implication that the state comes first; he wants a definition that suits the modern multiplicity of roles—we are not *just* citizens but lots of other things as well. Therefore, he seeks an understanding that fuses public virtue with the American interest in personal development, one that does not demand sacrifice of the self to the state but rather entails coming to see one's own interest as interwoven with the interests of others. Enlightened self-interest is inculcated not by the state itself but in mediating institutions like family, church, school, and neighborhood association.

Cooper argues that self-interest rightly understood—if rightly understood—need not imply selfishness. He suggests that we think of the self in self-interest as "complex, at once familial and communitarian"; to counter the usual image of isolated, competitive individuals, he offers Sampson's notion of "ensembled individualism," in which the self has permeable boundaries open to influence by other selves and groups—a form Cooper observes is more consistent with the "individualism" encountered in non-Western cultures and among feminists.

Cooper (1991, pp. 155-156) advocates self-interest rightly understood because, as he says, "self-interest seems as inescapable now as it did to de Tocqueville. The task is not to banish it, but to bound and humble it" (p. 157). But from whose perspective does self-interest appear so inevitable? The apparent pervasiveness of self-interest does not hold up to careful scrutiny. Cooper notes several authors whose research has called the ubiquity of self-interest in the public sphere into question. He does not, however, question the roots of the assumption, which lie in culturally masculine interests like competition, autonomy, and mastery; nor does he interrogate the paradox through which an ostensibly "universal" human characteristic fails to extend into the "haven in a heartless world"—the home. The inculcation of self-interest rightly understood depends on the existence of a realm that does not operate on premises that it makes any sense to call "self-interest," no matter how modified.

Cooper is, in fact, battling the fallacious reasoning that begins by assuming that human nature is innately selfish and then is stuck with redefining as some hybrid variant of self-interest all the behaviors that do not look or feel self-interested. We need "self-interest rightly understood" only if all human action must be thought of as in some way self-interested. The familial experiences of women (and of many men also) tell them that all behavior is *not* self-interested. If so, then perhaps it would make more sense—and would be more transformative along the lines Cooper seeks—to find models for virtuous citizenship in the realms where, according to his theory, it is to be fostered: in the home, the school, the church, and the neighborhood association. The difficulty, of course, is the reigning viewpoint that importing ways of thinking from the domestic or affiliative realm into the public is inappropriate—a perception that has barred for generations the ways of cultural womanhood from making any impact on public affairs. Feminist theorists have begun to make suggestions along these lines (for example, Ruddick's, 1989, "maternal thinking"), and I consider some of them in my final chapter. For now it is enough to point out that one cannot understand why Cooper's argument takes the form it does without understanding the masculinist roots of pillars of Western political thought like self-interest and the division between public and private.

CONCLUSION

This review of the gender dilemmas in ideas of virtue in public administration has identified several counts on which they must be considered masculinist. The underlying aim of these theories, to resuscitate the idea of public virtue to defend administrative authority, runs headlong into a gender-based division of social life into public and domestic sectors, a division that makes men primarily responsible for public affairs and women primarily responsible for domestic duties and the very terms of which have respectively masculine and feminine qualities. The nature of public life is that it is populated by independent, rational, autonomous men (or women "passing" as men), who protect the common good (sometimes merely by acting as referees among various claimants to public goods) and control the impulses of the people. Actors in the public sphere perform their duties out of enlightened self-interest to win fame in the eyes of the wise and the good (each other) and to go down in history. The nature of domestic life is to support life in the public sector—to provide the material conditions that make it possible for public life to go on, and to inculcate a concern for the common good. The existence of the public sector thus depends on there being another sphere in which reigning premises about human nature do not apply—one where virtue (benevolence, selflessness) rules and to which the desire for fame does not extend.

Advocates of the idea of public virtue therefore face the uphill task of bringing into public life a set of qualities that not only are thought not to apply there but that are seen as actively subversive of its premises—qualities that represent an incursion of the emotional, affiliative, selfless (therefore weak) feminine into the rational, enlightened, self-interested, autonomous masculine. It is not the idea of public virtue itself that is objectionable, but the assumption that we can have it without addressing an understanding of social life that divides existence, both conceptually and materially, into two different realms and privileges one (and its inhabitants) over the other (and its inhabitants). Certainly we cannot achieve public virtue as long as our images and exemplars reinforce the masculinist aspects of public life instead of undermining them. We must be willing to think new thoughts, to enter into Fisher's discovery process that makes a life that has no clear precedent, to invent the future not by building a hero factory but by building solidarity among people of similar aim, wherever we find them. We must be willing to be *thought* unrealistic. We must be willing to acknowledge the threads of womanhood within public administration and be prepared to weave a new fabric.

NOTES

1. The class bias in the idea of virtue continued, because it was higher-ranked and not poor women who came under its sway.

2. Lest it be thought that this is a phenomenon of the ancient past, recall that only in recent times have laws in *some* states been altered to prohibit husbands from raping their wives.

3. Adair (1974) notes that Alexis de Tocqueville saw many of the founding fathers as worshipers at the altar of "the bitch-goddess, Success, not in the Temple of Fame" (p. 22)—which, considering the roadblocks men have thrown in front of women's efforts to attain success on male terms, strikes one as an egregious projection and a bum rap, indeed, on the female sex.

6

From the Ground(s) Up:
Women Reformers and the Rise
of the Administrative State

Ideas about expertise, leadership, and virtue are blended in theories of public administration, and most arguments defending the administrative state draw on all three. For example, some writers justify the leadership of public administrators on the basis of their superior expertise and greater commitment to public service; others defend the public spiritedness of administrators in terms of the support that technical and managerial competence lends to their leadership; still others claim that administrative expertise is not simply technical but includes a more clear-sighted understanding of the public interest than we can expect of the average citizen and, therefore, justifies the exercise of discretion.

These themes began to emerge during the founding period of American government, when the constitutional fabric wove together strands that included the preeminence of the better sort (meaning both better educated *and* more respectable) and the need for energy in the executive. But they assumed new significance during the Progressive era, when reformers marshaled them in the interest of more active administrative government.

By focusing mainly on contemporary arguments, my critiques of expertise, leadership, and virtue may have created the impression that women played no part in the historical development of these images. On this basis the reader might be likely to conclude that reframing public administration from a perspective that embraces women's needs, circumstances, and interests will entail marrying two perspectives that have never been introduced to one another, so to speak. This discussion is intended to correct that impression by reviewing some of the highlights of the part women played during the late 19th and early 20th centuries (approximately 1880-1930), a time when the positive state developed and the self-conscious discipline of public administration took form. My aim is to suggest that the thinking and actions of women reformers shaped in important ways the emergence of the administrative state. On the basis of historical evidence, I argue that, although the field currently assigns them little weight, women's work and thought were crucial in shaping the understanding and practice of governmental reform. My argument is speculative at this point, because to date our knowledge of women's role in the history of public administration (rather than in the reform era generally) is sketchy. Nevertheless, the literature makes it possible to glimpse the outlines of the part women played.

My view of public administration as a product of Progressive reform is based on Waldo's now-classic treatment. Like Woodrow Wilson's essay, "The Study of Administration," Waldo's (1948) *The Administrative State* seems to have been widely ignored upon its publication; today, however, it is almost as difficult to imagine the field without Waldo as without Wilson. Waldo conceives of public administration as an ongoing struggle to reconcile or harmonize norms of democracy and efficiency (or, to put it in other ways, participation and expertise, values and science, politics and administration). Clearly this tension has been present since the founding era; one finds it, for example, in Hamilton's view that good government entails both "energy" (that is, effectiveness) and "safety" (or responsiveness to the people). But Waldo's analysis of Progressive thinking makes it clear that, partly because it led to a big increase in public administrative activity and partly because of the particular values it espoused, the Progressive reform movement raised the ante on the question of the relationship between democracy and efficiency:

> At the very heart of Progressivism was a basic conflict in social outlook. This conflict was between those whose hope for the future was primarily that of a planned and administered society, and those who, on the other hand, remained firm in the old liberal faith in an underlying harmony, which by natural and inevitable processes produces the greatest possible good if the necessary institutional and social reforms are made. (Waldo, 1948, p. 17)

Waldo notes that in practice public administration theory has privileged administrative concerns at the expense of democratic values. Interpretations by a number of subsequent students of the Progressive reform era are consistent with Waldo's. Wiebe (1967), for example, has suggested that the Progressive "search for order" began with the moral notion of purifying the urban machine to "cure" democracy but evolved to a quest for enduring social harmony that depended on the effective efforts of an efficiently functioning bureaucracy. Skowronek (1982) sees the period as characterized by a merger between "the traditional interests of virtuous gentlemen in a politics of deference . . . [and] the new policy interests [of] the social scientist and the expert," which turned "ideological conflicts into matters of expertise" (pp. 44, 166). Haber's (1964) study of the turn-of-the-century cult of efficiency conceptualizes the tension as one between ignorance-as-evil and intelligence-as-good. Wilson (1887/1978) himself, of course, couched the dynamic in terms of politics and administration, and achieved reconciliation through their separation, by means of the famous politics-administration dichotomy. Administrators would serve democracy's interests by leaving politics to legislators and concentrating on the neutral, expert execution of legislative dictates.

In assessing the tension between democracy and efficiency in the history of public administration, Waldo (1948) sounded themes that evoke the images of expertise, leadership, and virtue that we have seen are persuasive in the modern administrative state. His review of the *Bureau movement*, which promoted research into the workings of early-20th-century public agencies, summarizes these elements:

> The Bureau movement was a part of Progressivism, and its leaders were leaders of Progressivism. They were tired of the simple moralism of the nineteenth century, although paradoxically they were themselves fired with the moral fervor of humanitarianism and secularized Christianity. . . . They were sensitive to the appeals and promises of science, and put a simple trust in discovery of facts as the way of science and as a sufficient mode for solution of human problems. They accepted—they urged—the new positive conception of government, and verged upon the idea of a planned and managed society. They hated "bad" business, but found in business organization and procedure an acceptable prototype for public business. . . . They were ardent apostles of "the efficiency idea" and leaders in the movement for useful education. (Waldo, 1948, pp. 32-33)

As the following discussion shows, morality, science, "facts," positive government, business, leadership, and the efficiency idea, were all notions shaped during the Progressive era by the thoughts and efforts of women. These Progressive ideas cluster around the images reviewed in previous chapters, ideas that are still used to justify administrative authority: expertise (science, facts, business methods, efficiency), leadership (positive government, education of citizens, intelligent cooperation) and virtue (morality). I suggest that women reformers played a significant role in establishing the terms and symbols by which proponents would promote and later defend positive administrative government. By exploring the part women played, I hope to call attention not only to their contributions per se but to the gender dilemmas and paradoxes that came to inhabit these key ideas as they were shaped during a crucial period in the development of the American administrative state.

The main points I want to make, based on historical literature, are these:

1. During the 19th century, a privatized understanding of virtue, one associated with ideas about "true womanhood," obscured the public significance of women's charitable activities.
2. Before the expansion of the administrative state, the central tension between democracy and efficiency was foreshadowed in the struggle

of benevolent women to reconcile compassion for the needy with the increasing demand for businesslike methods in all areas of life.

3. Despite perception of female benevolent work as an aspect of domesticity, it was actually the precursor of many current governmental service functions. When the need for government to take on a leading role in the delivery of services to the needy became apparent, women were in the forefront of efforts to secure the transfer.

4. Despite women's key role in developing service activities later assumed by the state and in promoting the need for governmental activism, the persistently feminine image of virtue (hence of reform as well) led proponents of the administrative state to couch their arguments in culturally masculine terms that have since obscured women's important role in the rise of public administration.

TRUE WOMANHOOD

To understand the process and manner in which women influenced the development of the administrative state during the reform era, we must begin by considering how 19th century ideas about gender roles affected shared understandings of public and private virtue and how, despite being restricted by convention to domestic virtue and private benevolence, women's charitable activities were inherently public, both in location and significance.

I indicated in chapter 5 that the idea of republican motherhood during the Revolutionary period helped to privatize understandings of virtue by making the home the chief site of virtue and women its principal champions. In the first half of the 19th century this idea expanded into what has been called the "cult of true womanhood" (Welter, 1976) or the "cult of domesticity" (Kraditor, 1968). Cott (1977) describes this cultural phenomenon as follows:

Mother, father, and children grouped together in the private household ruled the transmission of culture, the maintenance of social stability, and the pursuit of happiness; the family's influence reached outward, underlying success or failure in church and state, and inward, creating individual character. . . . The emphasis placed on and agencies attributed to the family unit were new, and the importance given to women's roles as wives, mothers, and mistresses of households was unprecedented. The ministers, educators, and pious and educated women in the northern United States whose published writings principally documented this ethic made women's presence the essence of successful homes and families. Conversely, the "cult" both observed and prescribed specific behavior for women in the enactment of domestic life. (p. 2)

Cott points out that between 1780 and 1830 women's position in American society changed more profoundly than it had up to that time or would for the succeeding 50 years. The onset of industrialization, the spread of wage labor, and the consequent redefinition of work sharpened the distinctions between white men's and women's roles, a change reflected in the cult of domesticity. While for black women and men, almost all of whom were slaves, no practical distinction between home and work was possible, white women of modest means entered the labor force as textile workers and primary-school teachers, while the better off took on a variety of benevolent activities outside the home, such as visiting and caring for the sick and the poor, or threw themselves into causes including abolition, temperance, and women's rights.

Cott suggests that although these new pursuits might seem to contradict reigning ideas of womanhood and domesticity, women's enlarged activities actually depended on this ideology: Because the cult of true womanhood allocated a separate sphere to middle- and upper-class white women and assigned them a vocation within it, it gave them a sense of their own identity that provided the strength to claim new roles (Cott, 1977, pp. 4-9, 200-201).

At the same time, Ginzberg (1990) has argued, because ideas of true womanhood, with their overtones of domesticity and private benevolence, hid from people of the time the public significance of women's public-interested work, limitations on their formal political participation were easier to maintain and perceptions about the femininity of virtue could persist. Such dynamics have helped to obscure from historians of today—including those in public administration—the actual content of women's benevolent activities, their inherent publicness even while not formally associated with government, and their role as catalyst in the development of the positive state.

The centerpiece of the ideology of true womanhood was woman's moral superiority—her "piety, purity, submissiveness and domesticity" (Welter, 1976, p. 21), a premise that was used both to warrant woman's role as the moral guardian of home and society and to explain social phenomena such as the preponderance of males in prisons of the time (Ginzberg, 1990, pp. 12-13). The apparent gulf between woman's supposed moral excellence and the evils of society became the catalyst for the movement of women into social betterment activities: "The conviction that 'WOMAN,' as Sarah Hale put it [in 1855], was 'God's appointed agent of *morality*,' cemented the ideology of women's individual morality with the mandate to act to transform the world. . . . Women's agency was so gentle, pervasive, and unseen that the world would hardly know it was being subverted" (Ginzberg, 1990, pp. 14-15).

It is important to note that the idea of true womanhood was very much an elite white notion. Welter (1976) observes that women's benevolent work was supposed to be done out of pure affection and not for money or ambition: " 'True feminine genius,' said [writer] Grace Greenwood, 'is ever timid, doubtful, and clingingly dependent; a perpetual childhood' " (p. 29). Obviously relatively few white women, and virtually no black women, could afford to work outside the home without thought of money, and "perpetual childhood," distasteful as it seems to us today, has a connotation of privilege and self-indulgence that requires a good bit of income to support. Lerner (1979) points out that the onset of industrialization led to increasing differences in the types of work done by different classes of women:

> When female occupations, such as carding, spinning, and weaving, were transferred from home to factory, the poorer women followed their traditional work and became industrial workers. The women of the middle and upper classes . . . became ladies. . . . The image of "the lady" was elevated . . . [while] lower class women were simply ignored. (p. 25)

In addition, many white women were openly skeptical of whether true womanhood was attainable by African-American women even after emancipation. Freedwomen who sought to become homemakers were ridiculed as lazy instead of praised for their commitment to domesticity (Andolsen, 1986). Former masters and mistresses "would not agree to freedwomen 'playing the lady, being supported by their husbands like white folks' " (Sterling, 1984, p. xi). Race and class, therefore, limited participation in the cult of true womanhood to a relatively small proportion of women, whose comparatively privileged lives made them reluctant to find common cause with their less well off sisters (Allen, 1983; Andolsen, 1986).

What did charitable women actually do? According to Ginzberg, while women's benevolent organizations were generally separate from men's, this was not always the case, and—separate organizations or not—in actuality women and men did virtually the same work, including fund-raising, teaching, visiting the needy, and administration. Women as well as men sat on committees, prepared reports and leaflets, wrote letters, organized meetings, lobbied for legislation, and sought appropriations for their organizations. Because most white women reformers were married to men of considerable wealth and influence, they relied on these connections in lobbying and in gaining appointments to committees and commissions. Lacking such connections, women of color had to content themselves with providing services privately (Gordon, 1990, p. 24). Thus during a time when governments were little involved in what later came to be called *social welfare,* women were in the forefront of activity that set the stage for the moment when the need for the state to take the leading role would appear undeniable.

Ginzberg (1990) points out that women typically incorporated their charitable societies, a legal maneuver that enabled them to get around their own unequal status before the law (legally, married women were the wards of their husbands) and become, for practical purposes, legal "persons" who were not female. She suggests that "women's very interest in becoming incorporated challenges their insistence on a protected sphere" (p. 48). Incorporation also served to make women's benevolent activities appear more businesslike, an image that, as I discuss below, became increasingly important as the societal power of business corporations grew during the 19th century.

Men not only refrained from opposing women's charitable and reform activities but saw them as consistent with true womanhood, that is, with women's status as the inculcators of virtue. Because as nonvoters, women were legally defined as outside the public sphere, men saw female benevolent work as "above politics" (P. Baker, 1990, p. 63). Women's benevolence was natural, even when it extended to the institutionalization of their work, at first in private agencies, later in government itself. The mid- to late 19th century witnessed a growing assortment of such activities: "Besides the array of homes for wayward women, children, unemployed women, and destitute widows that sprouted up in antebellum cities, women increasingly founded industrial schools and houses of industry, establishments in which poor women earned wages in sewing and laundry rooms" (Ginzberg, 1990, p. 60). During and after the Civil War, women joined in government-sponsored relief work for soldiers and their families; for example, the Sanitary Commission, including its women's auxiliaries, provided food, clothing, and nurses for the war effort, and women allied themselves with state boards of charity that proliferated after the war to coordinate relief activities (Ginzberg, 1990, pp. 134, 196-197). In the latter part of the 19th century, white women's clubs established libraries and trade schools for girls, sponsored legislation to get rid of sweat shops and make tenements safer, pressed for a juvenile court system, and helped instigate measures for clean water and sewage disposal. Black women, of course, were barred from membership in "Progressive" circles (Neverdon-Morton, 1989). Their own clubs, set up at first to defend black men against lynching, soon expanded into a wide range of activities: forming kindergartens, nursery schools, day-care programs, orphanages and old folks' homes, and in general trying to make up for the lack of such institutions in or available to the black community, particularly in the South (Giddings, 1985; Lerner, 1979).[1] Despite the many spheres into which it extended and the important societal changes it wrought, however, women's charitable activity produced little change in widespread beliefs about their proper role. Their benevolence was still seen as private and an expression of domestic rather than citizen-like virtue.

BECOMING BUSINESSLIKE

While it began as an expression and symbol of feminine virtue, over the course of the 19th century women's philanthropic activity had to reshape itself in response to cultural developments.One was the growth of social science and the increasing emphasis placed on "facts" as the necessary basis not only for effective benevolent action but for the amelioration of social conditions of all sorts. It appears from historical studies that in some quarters the commitment to social science was seen as harmonious with women's interest and participation in betterment activities; in fact social science was perceived to be part of women's proper sphere. In 1874, Franklin Sanborn, secretary of the American Social Science Association, said that "the work of social science is literally women's work . . . but there is room for all sexes and ages" (quoted in Leach, 1980, p. 292). He referred to social science as the feminine side of political economy. Women could incorporate the concerns and methods of social science in their work because neither they nor men seemed to see them as inconsistent with benevolence based on moral sentiments.

Gradually, however, the feminine science of benevolent work took on increasingly masculine flavor that was at odds with women's existing habits of the heart. For example, Louisa Lee Schuyler, founder of New York State's Charities Aid Association, commented: "The efficiency of all associated effort depends largely upon good organization, the enforcement of discipline and the thoroughness of the work." Schuyler emphasized "obedience to rules," "esprit de corps," and other "soldierly qualities" (quoted in Ginzberg, 1990, p. 193), invoking norms the Civil War had made compelling but that also blended well with the scientific concern for order and proper procedure. Ginzberg observes that the demands of relief work during the war proved a watershed for benevolent activity, weakening earlier hopes of moral perfection, pointing up the need for systematic volunteer efforts, and replacing feminine sentiment with realistic, "manly exertion." Postwar philanthropy paid increasing homage to the more masculine values such as efficiency and science (Ginzberg, 1990, pp. 133-134), gradually coming to see systematic methods as ends in themselves rather than as instrumental to benevolence.

The masculinization of social science merged near the turn of the century with a broad social interest in efficiency (see chapter 3). The impact of the efficiency movement spread from women's public-spirited activities to the home itself, and women began trying to apply the dictates of scientific management to housework:

"Our hope is to bring the masculine and feminine mind more closely together in the industry of home-making by raising housework to the plane of Scientific Engineering," wrote one authority on domestic management. . . . The home was to be mechanized, systematized, . . . made free "from mere tradition and social custom." With drudgery banished from the household, the woman would be capable of assuming her equal role in society. . . . Elsewhere, the middle class mother was told to stop "soldiering" on her job, for the home was "part of a great factory for the production of citizens." (Haber, 1964, p. 62)

Thus not only did the cult of efficiency transform women's work in the public sphere, gradually replacing true feeling with concern for proper methods, it also invaded what had been thought of as an area of life beyond the reach of crass economic concerns.

Over the course of the century, two paradoxical developments stand out: Within the arena of charitable work itself, the institutionalization, corporatization, and professionalization of benevolent activities gradually suppressed the idea that women had anything unique (that is, moral sentiment) to bring to such pursuits; however, at the same time, in society at large, reform work as a whole came increasingly to be seen as feminine and ineffectual, particularly when contrasted with the vigorous masculinity of ballot-box politics. On the one hand, the increasingly businesslike approach to charity work demanded professional standards; from this perspective (as Schuyler's comment about soldierly qualities suggests), it was the absence of femininity—of softheartedness, of emotionality—that made a particular woman an effective charity worker. As Ginzberg (1990) notes, this denial of differences in style and circumstance between men and women both obscured real power differentials between the sexes and barred the development of radical insights that might have led to a reduction in sexual inequality. On the other hand, in the wider world the perception of virtue as a feminine (therefore soft and sentimental) characteristic reinforced the distinction between real—that is, partisan—politics and the nonpartisan reform movement. Party politics "provided entertainment, a definition of manhood, and the basis for a male ritual. . . . Party leaders commonly used imagery drawn from the experience of war . . . [and] commented approvingly on candidates who waged manly campaigns" (Baker, 1990, pp. 60-61). Party stalwarts disparaged reformers as politically impotent, calling them the "third sex" of American politics, "man-milliners," or "Miss Nancys" (Baker, 1990, p. 84 n.). From the party man's perspective, the effort to remove any aspect of government—for example, public administration—from politics seemed an effort to weaken, even to render impotent, the manly vigor of citizenship; similarly, the campaign for female suffrage threatened to wipe out an important distinction between women and men: "If women voted, they would abandon the home and womanly virtues: men would lose their manhood and women would begin to act like men" (Baker 1990, p. 69). Thus, in this instance as elsewhere, gender dynamics wrought a paradox that, regardless of the angle from which it is viewed, helped to maintain distinctions that worked to women's disadvantage. Where their perspectives and efforts had shaped an entire sphere of public-interested work (the sphere of benevolence), women's contributions came to be obscured by a rhetoric of professionalism that, as it denigrated moral feeling, rejected any difference in women's and men's approaches; on the other hand, in that arena of public life from which women were most firmly barred (electoral politics), a rhetoric of difference hindered women's attainment of full citizenship and preserved the notion of real politics as a matter of tough-minded masculinity.[2]

I have suggested that as women's benevolent work proliferated, the preferred approach became increasingly businesslike, a tendency that worked to obliterate any perceived value in the uniqueness of women's involvement. In fact, this encounter between women's benevolent activities and the dictates of efficiency and science is a harbinger of the tension between democracy and efficiency that Waldo (1948) sees at the heart of public administration theory (discussed above). In the development of public administration, Waldo argues, efforts to "harmonize" the two sets of values generally ended in efficiency taking precedence over democracy, particularly by insisting that there was really no quarrel between them: Facts would show the way, and among persons of intelligence in possession of facts there could be no serious disagreement. For example, Allen's (1907) *Efficient Democracy* declared: "Without . . . facts upon which to base judgment, the public cannot intelligently direct and control the administration of township, county, city, state, or nation. Without intelligent control by the public, no efficient, progressive, triumphant democracy is possible" (p. ix). But a similar clash had already occurred. In the case of women's public-spirited work, a set of moral values—the desire to help, to improve, to change—came up against demands for objectivity, efficiency, and science, and began to be absorbed by them. The need to be scientific and businesslike to appear competent could not be gainsaid. Benevolent work had to be systematized and professionalized, in order to be effective and to justify the expense and effort devoted to it; indeed, if the home itself could be seen as a "factory of citizenship" it would appear that the positive aspects of women's differences from men—those that could justify room in the public sphere for their charitable work—were in danger of being supplanted entirely in the public consciousness by those differences that were used to justify restrictions on women's social roles. Thus women could and did continue to play an important part in advancing reform causes, but under a rubric of social scientific efficiency that obscured the nature of their contributions. At the same time, public administration was developing during a period when benevolent and reform work were perceived as feminine in contrast to the vigor of party politics, a paradox that would lead male reformers increasingly to purge the new *science* of public administration of any taint of sentimentality—of femininity—by making sure that it was businesslike (see below).

SHAPING THE ADMINISTRATIVE STATE

So far in this discussion we have seen how ideas about the femininity of virtue and their expression in the benevolent work of white middle-class women shifted in response to the growing societal desire that such activities be efficiently conducted. I have argued that this effort to reconcile benevolence with expertise is a harbinger of the tension in public administration between democracy and efficiency. I want to turn now to the part women played in the rise of the administrative state, as their private charitable activities were transformed into governmental social service functions. The roots of the nascent administrative state in women's compassionate work with the needy and their more general interest in curing urban ills has been obscured partly due to a general tendency among historians to overlook women's contributions, but more important, because the feminine image of charitable work hid its public implications. I suggest that women's efforts to perpetuate and institutionalize their philanthropic activity, along with the perceptions they had about its social meaning, directly influenced the rise of the administrative state during the Progressive era. In a time when reformers as a group came increasingly to advocate that government play a leadership role in societal betterment, women reformers were in the vanguard, seeking to sustain forms of businesslike benevolence by securing government sponsorship of them. Because women saw the growing need for what we now think of as social services, a need whose scope they realized could only be handled by government, they deliberately sought both new policies and the administrative capacity to carry them forward. Thus women were notably responsible for the way in which threads of competence, virtue, and governmental leadership came together in the late 19th century to launch a major rationale for the administrative state.

Women had a number of reasons for their interest in perpetuating benevolent activities by turning them over to government sponsorship. For one thing, their activities had led them to broaden their understanding of the interrelationships among social problems and to see whatever initial concern had roused them to action as inextricably linked to a host of other problems, thus suggesting the need for more concerted efforts than could be undertaken by any one group of reformers. For example, members of the Women's Christian Temperance Union over time turned the demand for temperance, to which they had been spurred by witnessing the abuse poor women suffered at the hands of drunken husbands, into a fundamental critique of American society and a wider understanding of the public good (Baker, 1990, p. 68). In a similar way, women municipal reformers came to see the problems of cities in broad compass and to understand that the concerns of government were congruent with the concerns of women. Mary Beard (1915/1972) commented: "Having learned that effectively to 'swat the fly' they must swat its nest, women have also learned that to swat disease they must swat poor housing, evil labor conditions, ignorance, and vicious interests" (p. 221). In an argument reminiscent of self-interest rightly understood (see chapter 5), Carrie Chapman Catt's "Ready for Citizenship" observed:

City garbage collection is seen quickly to be a multiplication of many house garbage cans. City markets mean that the places where the individual housewife buys her children's food are multiplied many times over. Policy systems mean to her the safeguarding of the streets on which her children walk. The woman, more intimately than the man, finds government a matter related to her own work at every turn. (quoted in Andolsen, 1986, p. 49)

As Baker (1990) notes, once women realized that social problems had broad as well as local causes and were linked in complex ways that demanded more systematic efforts than a group of volunteers could accomplish, they began to shift the focus of their activities from personal involvement in charity work such as "friendly visiting" to lobbying for legislation in areas such as workmen's compensation, education, nutrition, and housing inspection (p. 71-72)—laws that would require governments to become involved directly in social betterment. Social science promoted this tendency by combining ideas of reform and betterment with a positive perspective on government (Leach, 1980). Social science "contributed a logic for joining forces with formal governmental institutions, because social science taught the importance of cooperation, prevention, and expertise" (Baker 1990, p. 68). Thus women reformers, motivated by moral and scientific concerns, played a key role in making the case for governmental leadership in social welfare.

The advent of woman suffrage greatly expanded and strengthened these lobbying efforts during the post-Progressive era. Lemons's (1973/1990) examination of *social feminism* identifies a number of important policy contributions women reformers were able to make once women's attainment of the vote made them (at least in prospect) a force in electoral politics. For example, the Sheppard-Towner Maternity and Infancy Protection Act of 1921 was, according to Lemons, "the first major dividend of the full enfranchisement of women"; its enactment was in large part the result of pressure by women's groups, who later fought successfully to keep it from being repealed (p. 153). But women also expanded their policy advocacy beyond traditional women's concerns. In the 1920s, the League of Women Voters studied the issue of public power in the United States and adopted a platform that included public ownership of the Muscle Shoals dam—the nucleus of what became the Tennessee Valley Authority (TVA). Their support was so crucial to the enactment of TVA that when President Roosevelt signed the bill into law in 1933, Belle Sherwin, president of the League, was the only nongovernmental person present (Lemons, 1973/1990, pp. 132-133). The League was also a leading proponent of civil service reform during the 1920s and 1930s. Its platform included

> reclassification based on job qualifications and skills, merit system for promotion, minimum wage in federal and state civil service, expansion of the classified service, enlargement of all civil service commissions to include representatives of employers, the general public, and administrative officials, and the delegation of full power to the commissions to maintain an efficient, non-political service. (Lemons, 1973/1990, pp. 134-135)

Thus women became involved not only in securing government sponsorship of service activities but in promoting policy on a wide variety of issues, including those that directly affected the capacity-building of public administration.

Fitzpatrick's (1990) study of four turn-of-the-century women social scientist reformers, all trained at the University of Chicago, illustrates the efforts of women intellectuals to use social analysis to stimulate social policy and to institutionalize reforms. Katherine Davis, who became the first superintendent of the New York State Reformatory for Women, advocated the scientific study of crime and corrections and helped to advance a new understanding of female delinquency. Frances Kellor did path-breaking research into the causes and results of unemployment and helped direct Theodore Roosevelt's 1912 Bull Moose campaign. Edith Abbott and Sophonisba Breckinridge did innovative investigations of urban problems, particularly economic barriers faced by urban women, and founded the first professional school of social work at a major research university, the University of Chicago. These women illustrate how individual women social scientists made their perspectives, interests, and talents an integral part of the growing interest in social policy per se—that is, in deliberate, coordinated, and institutionalized efforts to deal with social ills.

Thus when women came to see the need for concerted, large-scale betterment efforts, they were in the front ranks of those who advocated government policies and strategic action and were leaders in promoting a number of notable features of the early administrative state.

THE GENDER OF REFORM

Because public administration as a conscious enterprise developed during a time when virtue was seen as a feminine quality, male Progressives felt a need to make reform appear more muscular. Accused of being sissies by people they thought of as party hacks and rascals (definitely not persons the framers would have considered the better sort), the men of public administration responded by attempting to purge reform of any taint of sentimentality—of femininity—by making sure that it was seen as tough-minded, rational, effective, and businesslike. For example, W. Wilson (1887/1978) argued for the need to "strengthen and purify" government and saw administration not as a "mere passive instrument" but as necessarily imbued with "large powers." He ended his famous essay with the forecast that "if we solve this problem we shall again pilot the world" (p. 17). Goodnow (1900/1981) saw public administration as an "impartial and upright" endeavor that embraced "fields of semi-scientific, *quasi*-judicial and *quasi*-business or commercial activity" with "the most efficient possible" organization (pp. 88-89).

Perhaps the clearest expression of the reformers' effort to rid themselves of the taint of femininity can be seen in their explicit rejection of volunteer (i.e., largely female) benevolence. The comments of Bruere (1912/1981) are illustrative:

> The efficiency movement in cities . . . began . . . in an effort to capture the great forces of city government for harnessing to the work of social betterment. It was not a tax-saving incentive nor desire for economy that inspired this first effort . . . but the conviction that only through efficient government could progressive social welfare be achieved, and that, so long as government remained inefficient, volunteer and detached effort to remove social handicaps would continue a hopeless task. (p. 93)

Similarly, Charles A. Beard's openly masculine vision of the Bureau movement in municipal reform aimed to distinguish it on the basis of its strategic power from inchoate, natural (hence feminine) processes:

> If . . . I were compelled to state in a single sentence the most significant contribution of our movement to modern civilization, I should say that it is the application of the idea of continuous and experimental research, found so effective in economic enterprise, to the business of public administration—intimately and in a deep-thrusting sense, a contribution to the processes by which modern mankind is striving with all its resources to emancipate itself from the tyranny of rules of thumb and the blind regimen of nature, becoming conscious of its destiny as an all-conquering power. (quoted in Waldo, 1948, p. 33 n.)

CONCLUSION

In this chapter I suggested that our understanding of the development of the administrative state in thought and deed during the Progressive era is inadequate without awareness of the gender paradoxes that lie beneath the stories we ordinarily tell. We have seen that women's benevolent work was public both in its performance and its significance. Far from restricting themselves to wifely duties, both white and African-American women were notable presences in charitable activity. Over time this work led both women and men to see the need to expand the responsibilities of governments and those who could to work actively to stimulate governmental involvement. The tasks reformers sought to turn over to government had largely been considered women's work and seen as grounded in a peculiarly feminine virtue. As women's philanthropic work merged with the municipal reform effort, male reformers perceived the need to remove the taint of femininity that haunted reform (particularly in contrast to the muscular vigor of party politics) by ensuring that it was seen as businesslike and efficient—tough rather than sentimental. As long as social betterment was virtue personified and the persona was Woman, it could be perceived (despite obvious evidence to the contrary) as private. Because both the worlds of business and government were traditionally male, to make good works efficient by turning them over to reformed public administration was to make them masculine. The original rhetoric of difference (true womanhood) that had made women's benevolent work possible in the first place now had to be suppressed in favor of a rhetoric of professionalism and efficiency, large powers and the harnessing of forces. In the process, women's central place in an entire cultural-political phenomenon, the reform movement out of which self-conscious public administration emerged, was obliterated. Yet the tension between democracy and efficiency, between participation and professionalism, between values and facts, around which so much of the conversation in contemporary public administration revolves, shaped and was shaped by women's role in reform. The idea that the need for good management limits the feasibility of democracy in administration is essentially the same argument as the one reform women bowed to, namely that benevolence had to become businesslike to survive.

Among the lessons of this excursion into reform era history, then, are the unobserved gender dimensions of public administration's formative processes: How what we have thought of as neutral ideas like efficiency, businesslike methods, and the science of administration include problematic gender biases that are reflected in their historical development. Until we focus our attention on these matters, our justifications of administrative governance will continue to present women with insoluble dilemmas. Women do not simply represent "redecoration" of the house of public administration nor will they (we) be content to serve in this capacity. On the contrary, the project is not simply one of refurbishment but of reconstruction from the ground(s) up.

NOTES

1. The lives of 19th-century African-American women led them to see gender dynamics of the time in somewhat more trenchant terms than were apparently possible for even the most ardent white women reformers. As Carby (1986) notes, Anna Julia Cooper argued that white men's imperialist impulses were nurtured at home by white women preoccupied with maintaining their own economic privilege. Ida B. Wells maintained that the exalted moral status of white women served

as the basis for a campaign of fear and intimidation against black men that persisted for the better part of a century. White southerners gained northern tolerance of lynching by characterizing it as a response to the rape of white women by black men; Wells argued that the basis for this concession on the part of white northern men was their sense of ownership over white women's bodies. Carby (1986) observes:

> Wells['s] . . . analysis of lynching provided for a more detailed dissection of patriarchal power [than Cooper's], showing how it could manipulate sexual ideologies to justify political and economic subordination. . . . Cooper preferred to believe that what men taught could be unlearned [through] education. . . . Wells was able to demonstrate how a patriarchal system . . . used its control over women to attempt to completely circumscribe the actions of black males. (p. 309)

2. These dynamics have persistent echoes in our own time: The proper extent of women's public obligations (such as whether they should serve in combat during wartime) is still debated in terms that reveal persistent fear about obliterating the differences between men and women. For example, after the Persian Gulf war a William Buckley column commented that the spectacle of women on the battlefield was a threat to the civilized order that gives men the responsibility for protecting women.

7

Windows of Vulnerability,
Paths of Change

> The nation expects administrators to be on tap rather than on top, to be seen rather than heard, and to be loyal rather than assertive. . . . The consequence of such a posture is a servile, complaisant, compliant, and passive career service that presents itself as a window of vulnerability.
>
> Louis Gawthrop (1987)

The case for the legitimacy of the exercise of administrative discretion by unelected, tenured bureaucrats is an assertion of the right to rule—of the right to give binding answers to questions that shape the fates of people (sometimes great numbers of them) other than the ones directly involved in making the particular decision. As we have seen throughout this exploration, defenses of the administrative state generally ground the necessity for granting administrators this power in features of the political and economic context of public administration, such as advanced capitalism or interest group politics, that bespeak the need for control over events and processes. Sober reflections though they appear to be, these arguments are a defensive albeit low-key maneuver in a cultural battle over the role of government per se and the role of bureaucracy in particular. To combat popular disillusionment evoked by policy inertia and political scandal, and to counteract perceptions of bureaucratic incompetence, theorists have made the bold claim that administrative authority is necessary to accomplish public objectives, preserve crucial capacities, and promote important public values. The claim of legitimacy is a claim of rightful power.

Defending the American administrative state has always been a precarious enterprise, because of endemic popular suspicions about bureaucracy. After considering the gender dilemmas in these arguments, however, they seem even more problematic than has been generally apparent. Into prevailing debate over the justifiability of administrative discretion, this book has introduced considerations such as these: the correspondence between widespread ideas about masculinity and public administrative norms of professionalism and leadership; the extent to which bureaucratic structures and procedures, administrative career patterns, and the dynamics of public organizational life depend on women's disproportionate responsibility for domestic work; the administrative state's implication in sustaining gender roles that limit women's life choices; and the suppressed femininity of important administrative canons like responsiveness, service, and benevolence. In this book I have argued that the self-understanding of public administration, as reflected in its images of expertise, leadership, and virtue, is culturally masculine (although its masculinity is as yet unacknowledged), but that it also reflects a significant element of femininity (although consciousness of its femininity has yet to dawn). I have suggested that the masculinity of public administrative modes of thought privileges men and their interests by establishing boundaries on thought and action that exclude from positions of authority all but a relatively few "exceptional" women. My argument has pointed to conceptual dichotomies such as public/private and efficiency/democracy that not only work against the existing interests and needs of women but cannot be sustained on examination of actual practices. I have remarked on the tendency in public administrative thought toward heedless universalization, by means of which historically male practices and ideas are made to stand for humanity as a whole without any examination of their possible limitations where women are concerned. The discussion has also claimed that public administration theories emerge from and reinforce material realities that oppress women. These realities include the double burden of housework and paid employment that working women bear, their disproportionate relegation to the lower bureaucratic ranks, the glass ceiling that blocks their access to the positions of greatest power and monetary reward, and their lack of fit with organizational expectations about professional and managerial behavior.

In this final chapter I want to explore some of the implications of these gaps and paradoxes in public administration theory. My working assumption is that unease over public administration's vulnerability to public criticism (such as the Gawthrop quote above reflects) will not dissipate simply by fretting over its image of passivity and compliancy—no more than women have advanced their own liberation just by worrying about being seen as passive and compliant. The dichotomous nature of our thinking, the conviction that masculinity and femininity are mutually exclusive, sometimes leads us to leap to one extreme in an effort to avoid or deny the other. At a taken for granted level, passivity, compliance, and vulnerability are feminine, and in public life femininity is taboo. Therefore, public administrators, both women and men, seek ways to appear technically expert, tough, and heroic, when what we really ought to be doing is examining our simultaneous dependence on and denial of gender dichotomies. My belief is that only by exploring public administration's gender dilemmas, instead of denying their existence, will we begin to develop a form of public administration that merits public approbation. Only then will we find paths that lead us toward change.

To begin this project of using gender to reshape public administration theory, we need to think about what a feminist theoretical stance might be and about some of what feminist theorizing might produce. On both counts, the following observations can only be suggestive of what must be myriad possibilities and are meant to serve simply as a catalyst. I begin with some general observations on the nature of feminism and feminist theorizing, then reprise the critiques from earlier chapters in the process of making specific initial suggestions about how to bring feminist theory to bear on ideas of competence, leadership, virtue, the history of public administration, and the nature of the administrative state. The book concludes with a more sustained examination of one normative theory of public administration—administrative discretion as *phronesis,* or practical wisdom—as an example of the transformative potential that lies in feminist theorizing.

A FEMINIST APPROACH TO THEORY

Feminism has apparently acquired something of a bad name over the last decade or so. In countless conversations with women in public administration during this period, I have encountered over and over the following paradox: Although most women I talk with firmly support equal pay for equal work, equal access to jobs (including those at the top), the sharing of housework, and better child-care facilities, and many are interested in promoting culturally feminine qualities in the workplace, they are very likely to dissociate themselves from "feminism," which they equate either with academic abstraction or with shrill narrow-mindedness and even man hating. When I asked during a recent conference panel discussion whether the ideas of Mary Parker Follett might today be considered feminist, several women made it clear that they saw *feminist* as an undesirable characterization both for Follett and themselves, although one woman I spoke to afterword admitted that as far as she knew she had never read a feminist book. Faludi (1991) may be right that many women's current distaste for the feminist label is the result of a cultural backlash against the gains women made during the "second wave" of feminism, a reaction that has raised the cost of counting oneself a feminist. At any rate, it seems clear that an argument like mine that seeks to have an impact beyond the walls of academe runs a risk by introducing this controversial term into the discussion. It seems especially important, therefore, to define what I mean by it.

The first thing to say is that most feminist theorists today no longer believe that it is possible or even desirable to settle on one definition of feminism. Many theorists now speak of "feminisms" as a way of acknowledging and even celebrating the diversity of viewpoints among women who wish to take the impact of gender dynamics into account in understanding the world. Women of color have been a major factor in moving feminist theory toward this pluralist position, but the tendency has been reinforced by the widespread realization that to universalize one version as *the* feminist worldview would be to replicate the fallacy of over-generalization pervasive among male thinkers, in which observations and reasoning based in elite white men's experiences and concerns are applied equally to women, people of color, working class and poor people, and so on.

What, then, does the term *feminism* entail today? To what does it commit the person who speaks as a "feminist"? Three things, in my view: to the proposition that gender is a crucially useful category of analysis, to a critical perspective on women's current status and prospects, and to use Gerda Lerner's words, to "a system of ideas and practices which assumes that men and women must share equally in the work, in the privileges, in the defining and the dreaming of the world" (quoted in Astin & Leland, 1991, p. 19).

With those propositions in mind, the most fundamental way to characterize a feminist approach to theory is to say that, because the gender lens encourages one to see the underlying assumptions (experiential and otherwise) that shape concepts and conclusions, feminists tend to see theory not as instrumental but as constitutive (Ferguson, 1984). Rather than being a tool to develop and then apply to an out there reality, the way one applies a wrench to a bolt, theory brings the world into focus—it makes the world, and thus shapes action in the world. Theory organizes the world, bounding the flow of its lived duration into packages or arenas and interpreting relations among them that we can think about and out of which we can make sense of our experience. The making of meaning depends on establishing conceptual boundaries between things—on being able to discern differences among them. Thus coherence entails limits; but limits also create new possibilities, for boundaries can be breached or subverted or redrawn, or we can reach beyond them (Cocks, 1989).

The conceptual boundaries established by theory—the world they create—are a kind of power, in the sense of force as well as the sense of enablement or capacity. "The limits of what people can think sets the limits of what they can do" (Cocks, 1989, p. 30). Therefore when we come to agreements about which considerations appropriately lie within or outside a particular theoretical arena, we also set limits on the lived experience of people who inhabit the form of life in question. The way we frame a theoretical conversation not only makes a certain kind of coherence possible but establishes an orthodoxy that literally keeps us from being able to hear certain voices that have been defined as not parties to the dialogue because they raise issues that do not fit or belong. Once during a meeting of public administration theorists I heard a well-known and respected figure say that he wanted a "structured public argument" that would make certain questions "off limits"—an unusually frank and self-aware declaration of a strategy by which intellectuals in disciplines achieve, beyond specific conceptual wrangles, a definitional or metatheoretical level of like-mindedness that keeps the world from being turned upside down. But the insistence on maintaining these established boundaries (similar to what Kuhn, 1970, calls a paradigm) is at the same time a strategy of legitimation *and* a strategy of suppression—a flexing of cognitive muscle that has not only conceptual but material consequences. For example, when questions of gender or race are seen as irrelevant to public administration theory, many of the greatest needs and interests of people whose lives have been fundamentally shaped by their racial and/or gender identities are eliminated from view. Their voices are silenced, unless they are willing to speak a language in which there is no room for certain of their most urgent concerns.

A feminist approach to public administration theory entails calling these boundaries into question and exploring their implications, which include the material differences in access to resources and power they sustain and the perceptions of self and world they generate. From the feminist perspective, it is a piece of luck that conceptual boundaries have never been completely impermeable. Because what *is* can only be understood in relation to what *is not*, the stronger the effort to set limits, the more such efforts depend on keeping near at hand that which has been excluded. Whatever is "other" always manages to infiltrate a particular community of knowledge, because coherence relies so thoroughly on the ability to discern difference (Johnson, 1987). *Otherness* exists in the interstices of the most firmly constructed body of theory—and public administration is far from the sturdiest of these. Thus the feminist approach involves focusing attention on the paradoxes, inconsistencies, and contradictions *within* public administration theory, as much or more than it does on opening up theory to something that currently lies outside it.

Like all knowledge, both public administration theory and feminist theory are rooted in certain interests (Habermas, 1971), in the sense either of material resources, a claim to share in some social good, or simply a particular absorption and curiosity. Feminism's chief interest is in the liberation of women. Although feminists vary in their approach to this project, they are in general agreement that feminism is not just one or a cluster of theoretical positions among many, but a politics. Although issues of color and class still produce divisions and controversies, women are beginning to find common cause in the struggle to end their subordination whatever its basis rather than in theoretical agreement about its source or about the nature of gender dynamics in particular racial and ethnic groups.

Having had the terms of women's lives and interests ignored, obliterated, or deprecated by male theorists, feminists tend to come at theorizing from a standpoint that emphasizes the particular over the universal, tolerates ambivalence and difference, and tries to encompass dichotomies instead of getting caught on one side of them. Feminists observe that dichotomies are rarely between equal terms; instead, one term assumes preeminence over the other. For example, Western theory privileges mind over body, culture over nature, public over private, thought over feeling, man over woman (of course, these are aspects of the same dichotomy rather than different ones—thus what appear to be purely conceptual hierarchies actually reflect material conditions). Feminists want to speak in terms of difference rather than dichotomy and to make room for varied points of view and for claims specific to particular experiences—hence the stress in this book on the ways in which generalizations about expertise, leadership, and virtue in public administration are inconsistent with women's diverse experiences in the world of administrative practice. In their encounter with other bodies of theory, including public administration, feminists want to engage with the conceptual traditions they seek to transform. This move involves not wiping out what exists but to use elements of it to make something better (Young, 1987)— to expand, turn inside out, or otherwise reshape aspects of existing theory as well as to sound new themes. To some feminists this project seems like an effort to say things for which there are no words, so thoroughly has male-generated theoretical language (because of its tendency to universalize masculine perceptions and concerns) precluded speaking from any woman's perspective (e.g., Landes, 1989). Others note that womanhood is a problematic location from which to try to speak because it is neither biological nor archetypal but a function of unequal power relations (e.g., Ferguson, 1984; Young, 1987). Nor do we know what either men or women would be if neither felt compelled to be preeminently what the other was not. Because we do not know what we might become, therefore, having no experience of a nonsexist society to suggest it, feminists are committed simply to women's process of becoming and the struggle to remove impediments to it, both conceptual and material—that is, to liberation.

TOWARD A FEMINIST THEORY OF PUBLIC ADMINISTRATION

Because feminist theorizing is like trying to think in a language that does not yet exist, that cannot exist while women are subordinated, delineating the substance of a feminist theory of public administration is a matter of catching glimpses of what might be rather than setting forth a full-blown vision. As French feminist Julia Kristeva observes, political reality makes it necessary to struggle in the name of women even as we acknowledge that under current circumstances a woman can exist only as her refusal of that which is given: "I therefore understand by 'woman' . . . that which cannot be represented, that which is not spoken, that which remains outside naming and ideologies" (quoted in Moi, 1985, p. 163). A feminist theory of public administration, as something that *must* be even though it cannot yet be, begins by identifying the "windows of vulnerability" that have the potential to become small paths toward change, the tiny points of entry through which considerations of gender have infiltrated existing theory simply because of its dependence, in order to be coherent, on saying what it is not. As Johnson (1987) puts it, womanhood is the "uncanny alien always already in the house"; the relationship between the alien and the master of the house (between woman and man) is that "each is already inhabited by the other as a difference from itself" (p. 35). In this sense, public administration does indeed have windows of vulnerability, and I have tried to identify some of them in this book: elements in defenses of public administration that reflect gender paradoxes and contradictions, and threads (threats?) of womanhood that run through the history and current practice of public administration. I have argued that public administration at once depends on and denies the existence of womanhood—both the life circumstances of actual women and the unacknowledged gender dimensions of concepts like professionalism, leadership, virtue, service and responsiveness.

What of the paths toward change? Perhaps we can discern them by reconsidering some of the paradoxical concepts raised in earlier chapters, to discover neglected dimensions, reflection on which might bear fruit.

Expertise. We saw that current ideas about bureaucratic competence stress a neutral objectivity that depends on a separated self mastering nature and sees the ideal form of knowledge as hard data; this sort of objectivity supports the individual liberty valued in liberal philosophy by making the state a neutral arbiter among competing claims. The feminist perspective, however, reveals this model of knowledge to be anything but neutral, because of the centuries-old association between nature and woman, and because the liberal state depends on the subordination of women. I argued that forms of neutrality like the Brownlow Report's passion for anonymity or the Blacksburg Manifesto's agency perspective depend heavily on the ability of the individual administrator to identify with the constructed filigree of interpreted values, practices, and perceptions that comprise a particular agency, which are a function of its history and prior membership. Dependence on the compatibility between agency perspective and individual identity puts a premium on similarities of life experience, including those rooted in gender, race, and class, that poses a dilemma for women and others who are different from the agency norm.

On a theoretical level, a feminist interpretation of the agency perspective would entail, first, acknowledging the partiality of what has been considered neutral (hence universal); in other words, feminism would argue for developing a sociology of agency knowledge and values in which gender, race, and class are major considerations. Such a move would dispel the notion that the agency perspective takes shape in a cultural vacuum. An agency cannot be sure of its ability to ascertain the "widest possible interpretation of the public interest" if its judgments are circumscribed by the values and experiences of a relatively narrow range of humanity. Nor can theorists argue confidently for the legitimacy of agency interpretations of the public interest without exploring how to transform limited perspectives into ones that truly take diverse points of view into account. On a practical level, continuing efforts to diversify agency staffs through affirmative action and pay equity policies will support a diversity-based public interest, but not unless the agency culture is such that all agency members are both unafraid to bring to bear their own life experiences and values on agency thinking *and* committed to a group process that will transform individual perspectives into something that is both diverse and universal and thus can be justified as the public interest. Confronted with race and gender diversity in their membership, institutions, including public agencies, have a way of trusting the universality of established values and practices while seeing as biased the new ideas injected as the result of an increasingly diverse work force. Lowering barriers to people who were previously discriminated against entails lowering barriers to the possibility that their ideas will work material changes in business as usual.

At present, our ideas of expertise also include autonomy, a notion that is in tension with the public servant's obligation to be politically responsive. Theorists portray an administrator who is an agent, not simply the extension of another but one who acts on behalf of another in the absence of specific orders, a balancing act that I suggested has suppressed gender dimensions given the cultural association between femininity and such ideas as responsiveness or being the extension of another. The separated self is visible here too, blocking the kind of connection and affiliation with the world that would make faithful efforts to reflect the needs of those whom one serves a source of pride rather than a sign of weakness. From the feminist perspective, the idea of expertise would put much more emphasis on the ability to establish connections of empathy and understanding, without denying the need for an ability to think and judge independently.

Ideas of objectivity and autonomy not only separate the individual from the field but they also raise the administrator above the field. Professional competence reduces those over whom authority is exercised to a state of dependence: Expertise depoliticizes the claims of clients, discounts the value of citizens' views, and dissociates itself from nonprofessional workers. From the feminist perspective, we need a form of competence that is nonhierarchical: professionals who rather than seeing their own knowledge as preeminent believe that all parties to the situation at hand—clients, citizens, other workers—have perspectives that are necessary parts of the whole, without which the widest possible public interest cannot be ascertained.

Finally, we need a form of competence in public administration that moves beyond the myth of the heroic male professional who sacrifices "selfish" family concerns in single-minded fashion to his career. The difficulty is not only that most women find it difficult or impossible to live up to such an ideal but that the ideal itself is warped, in that it compartmentalizes life and the men and women who live it, relegating the family to lesser status and performance of its responsibilities to lesser people. From the feminist perspective, the legitimate public administrator will be a whole person, one who is understood to have developed in and to be a continuing member of a family; the work of agencies will be seen as supporting and supported by the wider dimensions of its members' lives, and agency personnel policies will reflect this understanding. Politics such as parental leave and on-site day-care facilities will be seen (just as public schools are seen) as in the public interest because they promote the nurturing and development of children; they will not be viewed solely as meeting the needs of individual employees.

Once in a while, one can catch a glimpse of difference in current theoretical work on expertise; for example, Morgan and Kass's (1991) stewardship model of public administration encompasses the possibility that administrative expertise may sometimes extend to acting as "the midwives of constitutional change" (p. 52). The authors do not explore any of the dimensions of this metaphor—but what if we took it seriously? What would it mean if we made room for a thoroughly domestic idea and thought of administrators as midwives instead of as autonomous agents, above and detached from ordinary life? The image of the midwife is of a skilled and caring person who facilitates the emergence of new possibilities by means of embodied and embodying action. The good midwife has deep knowledge and vast experience, which she brings to bear on each unique situation, using them to help her sense the nuances of a process that she can only facilitate rather than steer. The process is an embodied, life-or-death affair (no distanced contemplation here!), one on which she brings to bear both her own body and her mind, one that requires *both* connection and a certain level of detachment *in order to be of greatest service.* In terms of models of competence, public administration could learn much from the midwife.

Leadership. In reviewing ideas and images of leadership in public administration, I argued that, in light of the lack of research evidence linking it with organizational outcomes, leadership should be considered an ideology that rationalizes (among other power relations) existing role expectations based on gender, race and class. Cultural ideas about leadership match notions of white professional male behavior and serve as a filter to keep most people who do not conform to these expectations from becoming leaders.

Images of leaders are questionable from the feminist perspective. We saw, for example, that just as the operation of vision distances the one who looks from the objects in view, the visionary leader objectifies and asserts control over others in the organizational situation. In the image of the leader as decision maker, emphases on taking charge, being task oriented, exerting authority, and maximizing rational efficiency all suggest that people "need" to be led and that participatory process is purely an instrument in the achievement of organizational goals, if not a reflection of the leader's weakness. Images of the inspirational or symbolic leader are based on the assumption that, regardless of their own self identities, people find it equally easy to identify with or emulate warriors and father figures. Because of the cultural masculinity of these images of leadership and because in actual fact most of the people viewed as leaders are men, women who move into leadership positions encounter the problem of whether to display characteristics that will mark them as inappropriately masculine or strive for a softer image and risk being seen as indecisive. Thus women are faced with the task of managing their gender, a problem male leaders do not have to try to solve.

From a feminist perspective, one obvious solution to the dilemma with which accepted leadership images present women is to move increasing numbers of women into leadership positions, in the hope that over time as women leaders become less rare there will be a shift in our norms of leadership. Absent a more thorough-going attention to the masculinity of organizational dynamics, and faced with research results that suggest little real difference between men's and women's leadership styles *in conventional organizations*, feminists question whether simply adding women in key positions will be enough to bring about so fundamental a change. But feminists would also want to raise the question of whether feminine leadership styles simply mask hierarchy more effectively; they would want to explore whether we need leaders at all—in the sense of someone who defines the meaning of situations, shows others the right way to approach problems, and makes them want what the leader wants (motivates them). From this perspective, it may be that the perceived need for leadership is a function of hierarchy, which socializes those in the lower ranks to believe that they are incapable of contributing to a joint effort to decide what to do, or that if they do have viewpoints, they had better follow the chain of command. Kelley's (1989) ideas, although not ostensibly feminist, are consistent with what many feminists would advocate. He suggests that people in work settings form into small leaderless groups in which each member of the group assumes equal responsibility for achieving goals, or alternatively, that groups rotate the leadership role. He notes: "Some of these temporary leaders will be less effective than others, of course, and some may be weak indeed . . . [but] experience of the leadership role is essential to the education of effective followers" (Kelley, 1989, p. 133).

Existing organizational norms of efficiency will make forming and sustaining leaderless groups heavy going. Conventional wisdom sees hierarchy as the inevitable form for complex organizations in postindustrial society, a view that blocks consideration of alternative forms and practices as impractical or unrealistic. Even discussions of the new entrepreneurial, flexible, participative form of management assume that there will have to be a leader to keep the mission on track, and most of the delegation and decentralization that goes on is carefully restricted. In addition, most organizational members continue to be somewhat uncomfortable with the structureless feeling a leaderless group evokes. In teaching, I have observed that when I ask my classes to decide how to organize themselves, even 10 minutes of time (out of a 3-hour class) spent working out a process that everyone can live with begins to seem like a waste of time to many members of the class, and I find myself growing internally nervous about being seen as indecisive. Thus I am aware of how far we are in complex organizations from being able to practice ideas like leaderless groups or rotating leadership. I do believe, however, that if we were to cease assuming, even for a little while or in a limited arena, that organizations or societal systems "need" leadership, we might make room for some fresh perspectives to emerge. In public administration, putting a hold on such assumptions might give us the opportunity to question the power implications in ideas about the need for administrators to lead a system of government that, from the bureaucrat's perspective, may appear fractionated and inefficient, but that from the perspective of ordinary citizens is much more likely to seem like a monolithic juggernaut. Could we make room, for example, for an image of administrative leadership that includes facilitating a share in organizational decision-making for agency clients, for citizens, and for secretaries and clerks?

Virtue. The feminist perspective on virtue takes a somewhat different tack from the revisions of competence and leadership. In the first two cases, the problem was one of cultural masculinity masquerading as universality, blocking nonconforming people and their ideas. In discussions of virtue in public administration we do find masculine images—the guardian, the seeker of fame, the hero—but in the idea of virtue itself we can perceive a latent femininity that these images unconsciously attempt to mask. The refashioning of American ideas about virtue during the founding period transformed it from a culturally masculine quality expressed in the public actions of republican citizens to a trait inculcated by women in the home and practiced in private acts of benevolence. This transformation of virtue feminized it, particularly in contrast to the masculine assertive pursuit of rational self-interest in the world of business. In order for public administration to resuscitate the notion of *public* virtue, then, masculine images have been brought to bear. The guardian or protector of the people is a father-figure, turning the unruly masses into a loyal and obedient flock. The Hamiltonian seeker of fame and honor is a paternal, ambitious, and Olympian actor before a public audience, dependent on women to handle necessities like food and child rearing but repressing their significance in favor of a quest for immortality. The hero is typically a commanding figure with a masculinity that extends back to the time of the ancient Greeks.

From a feminist perspective, the idea of virtue will remain problematic as long as the dependence of the public sphere on the domestic—and the sexual division of labor that goes with it—goes unacknowledged. Publicness, including public virtue, has excluded and silenced women for centuries. The public space has been a male preserve, a reality that made it possible for the American founders to enthrone self-interest and expel virtue by associating the one with men and the other with women. *Public virtue* thus involves a reuniting of masculinity and femininity. Unless we are able to approach the project of promoting the virtue of public administrators in light of that assumption, we will continue to struggle with the apparent "weakness" of virtue: It will continue to seem soft, sentimental, or (most damning charge of all) unrealistic.

Of all the current images of the public administrator, the idea of the administrator-as-citizen comes closest to an understanding consistent with a feminist perspective; however, this feminist, at least, would want to move Cooper's idea of the administrator as "citizen for the rest of us" to "citizen *with* the rest of us." Why could we not come to see the place of the public administrator in American governance as special not for its elevation but for its centrality? Based on such a vision, public administrators deserve our approbation not because they understand the public interest better than the rest of us but because they are willing to bear more of the burden for facilitating its accomplishment. As *facilitators,* their role is to make the governance process as inclusive as possible, particularly of those whose interests and needs are poorly represented in interest group politics (Stivers, 1990a). To fulfill this role, the administrator-as-citizen sees herself or himself as *partner with* rather than "guardian of" or "citizen for"—one who occupies a location in the web of government that gives her or him not only access to sharable information but also a boundary-spanning capacity, both of which can be used to empower others (Stivers, 1990b).

Like the midwife in the case of expertise, a domestic image that might re-unite public and private images of virtue is Ruddick's (1989)idea of motherhood as "fostering growth," or "nurturing a child's developing spirit." Ruddick argues that children require this nurturing because of the *complexity* of their developmental process; she points out that the central maternal tasks entailed in fostering growth are *administrative,* requiring the organization of effort in the face of the many destabilizing influences in children's lives. Ruddick argues that, while the fostering of growth entails a great deal of routine, sometimes exhausting work, it is at the same time fascinating and rewarding. Ruddick suggests that fostering growth requires a "metaphysical attitude" that both holds close and welcomes change, one that sees children as "constructive agents of their world and their life in it" (pp. 82-93). Thus we have a maternal image that matches in many ways the lives and responsibilities of virtuous public administrators: Like mothers, they must foster growth under conditions of complexity; like mothers, they must perform both routine and rewarding work in the interests of others who are in a sense their responsibility; like mothers they must both hold close (conserve administrative resources and capacities) and welcome change; just as mothers must see their children as agents of their own lives, so must public administrators see citizens.

The general emphasis in the feminist perspective is on such horizontal rather than vertical relations: on *seeing oneself* as reaching across rather than down, on *seeing others* as respected equals rather than threats to one's own autonomy or sheep in need of herding. This perspective also entails viewing the conceptual division between public and domestic spheres as permeable and mutually supportive. The intention here is not to promote governmental control over the intimate aspects of our lives—for indeed, a seemingly hard and fast line between public and private has never prevented governments from controlling the bodies of women, it has only rationalized the exclusion of women from public life. Instead the intent is to make explicit the reliance of governance—of individual and group action in public—on the support that governing (in fact all) individuals receive (or are presumed to receive) at

home: the shelter, food, clothing, rearing, nurturing, and comfort that make life livable. Awareness of the mutuality of public and domestic spheres should lead us to demand equal sharing of the work in the two sectors by men and women, thus to understandings of them (sectors and sexes) as equally important. As long as public administrators assert their rightful share in ruling a special public sphere that depends on but denigrates the domestic, they will be laying claim to a sphere that puts women in their place and perpetuating a weak understanding of virtue.

History. We saw that women played an integral role in 19th-century benevolent work and in governmental reform efforts, both of which were significant forces in the development of the administrative state. When turn-of-the-century governments began to take on new responsibilities, much of what they began to do was women's work (social service), and it was at women's behest (at least significantly so) that they began to do it. Although giving women's involvement in the history of public administration its due is certainly important, its significance extends beyond women's role in history to the conceptual shift that such awareness necessitates. We see that historically the central tension in public administration between values (benevolence, democracy, the public) and techniques (efficiency, administration) is pervaded with gender implications: That just as reform women sacrificed their uniquely feminine approach to charitable work in an effort to live up to standards of businesslike practice, so public administration sacrifices democracy at the altar of efficiency. In the accepted way of things, the ultimate *practical* (practitioner's) question becomes: How much participation (or process, or feeling) can we afford?

Thus a feminist approach to public administration entails a reexamination of its history, not only to give women their rightful due as full participants in setting the administrative state on its course but to understand the gender dimensions implicit in its most central ideas and the interests that are thereby served. As Scott (1989) observes, history, which is preeminently the history of politics and government, has been "enacted on the field of gender" (p. 100). Gender is both "a constitutive element of social relationships" (p. 94) and "a primary field . . . by means of which power is articulated" (p. 95). If so, it is clear that public administration, as both a configuration of social relationships and an institution of public power, needs gender as a category of analysis in order to be more fully delineated. Just as we now accept the impossibility of understanding the practice of public administration stripped of its political and economic context, so we must recognize that attention to the influence of gender, class, and race are fundamental to comprehension not only of present-day conceptual configurations but of their lineage, their historical development. Clearly, implicitly gendered ideas have contributed to defenses of the administrative state since its inception. A feminist approach to the history of public administration and its theory is thus not a matter of interest only to women (and thus relegated to the realm of women's studies) but central to a full understanding of the field.

Case in point: the gender dimensions in the tension between efficiency and democracy, revealed in the Progressive era spectacle of womanly benevolence invaded by masculine (businesslike) methods and in men's efforts to purge reform arguments, such as those in favor of administration, of any taint of sentimentality. Although theorists of public administration tend to treat the democracy-efficiency issue as a matter of rational argument, the lens of gender would suggest that the rationality of the discussion is "bounded," to use Herbert Simon's well-known term, but in a manner that has not yet occurred to Simon. It may be that the tendency in public administration to treat democracy as a cost of doing business, tolerable only to the extent that efficiency allows (as in, How much participation can we afford?), reflects nonconscious homage to masculinity. In the absence of this awareness, proponents of democratic administrative practice will continue to have difficulty explaining why persuasion that appeals solely to cognitive capacities continues to have so little effect.

Another implication of women's part in the history of public administration has to do with coming to terms with diversity. History suggests that integrating gender—as well as race and class—into thinking in public administration will entail more than simply bringing difference into the fold—that is, turning it to the service of administrative interests, conventionally defined. During the 19th-century women's philanthropic activities came under increasing pressure to become efficient and were finally absorbed by an administrative state that viewed efficiency with reverence. Ever since, womanly benevolence has been frequently on tap but never on top; thus one side of a dichotomy took control of the other, requiring it to subsume its nature in order to survive. A gender analysis of public administration's history, then, suggests that dealing effectively with what appear to be either-or choices will involve what Follett (1918/1965) calls an "interweaving of willings" (p. 69). Follett, the one authentic grand old woman of public administration, viewed diversity not only as inevitable but as a positive force in life. She argued that it was a great mistake to try to get rid of diversity: "fear of difference is dread of life itself. . . . One of the greatest values of controversy is its revealing nature. The real issues come out in the open and have the possibility of being reconciled" (Follett, 1924/1951, p. 301). Follett would tell us now, I believe, that public administration needs to risk a truly open dialogue, one in which differences are encouraged rather than papered over, one that therefore constitutes "co-creating . . . [that is,] the core of democracy, the essence of citizenship" (p. 302).

The Administrative State. Women's perspective on the administrative state is much more likely to be developed sitting in the secretarial pool or facing the caseworker's desk than it is as a member of the Senior Executive Service. A feminist approach to public administration necessitates examining the material realities of women's place in the bureaucracy and the barriers they face to more diversified participation. Thinking about personnel policies cannot confine itself to issues such as how to respond to "employee demands" for day care (as if the adequate care of children had no public interest dimension), or to facile comments about how much the agency relies on its support staff (without paying them in line with the level of its dependence). We must move to an investigation of how a refusal to take such material realities into account has limited our thinking. Because much of the management literature in public administration journals and textbooks evinces no consciousness that there are two sexes in organizations or that their respective experiences are in any way different, the opportunities for new approaches are limitless. We need to start by changing the tone of discussions about the "diverse work force," from considering it a looming problem to thinking of it as a promising new capacity. Next we might spend time reflecting on (instead of denying) the existence of sexual dynamics in the bureaucracy, as well as the extent to which conscious or unconscious racism and sexism hinder the progress of diverse employees and block changes in the terms of organizational life. No public manager should practice without becoming educated about these issues and without developing awareness of his or her personal implication in them. No theorist should develop a model of managerial excellence that does not include sensitivity to and skill in dealing with gender issues, including the disparity between norms of expertise and leadership and expectations about proper sex role behavior as well as the dilemma it poses for women managers.

In addition, a feminist perspective on the administrative state would encourage theory to come to terms with depersonalized power. The claim to exercise administrative discretion is the claim to power on the basis of technical, managerial, and moral expertise. The discretionary judgments of administrators are said to be justifiable because they make decisions on the basis of more objective knowledge, clearer vision, or higher principles than other citizens. This claim to power is asserted on the basis that the arena in which it is exercised is distinctive because public. But as we have seen, a discrete public sector maintains its boundaries (therefore its exceptionalism) at the expense of women. A feminist interpretation of administrative discretion and of the power inherent in it must, therefore, begin by calling into question the accepted model of discretionary judgment.

FEMINIST PRACTICAL WISDOM

The idea of discretionary judgment provides a good opportunity to explore in more depth the theoretical implications of feminism in public administration, because it draws together themes of competence, leadership, and virtue that have permeated this examination of public administration theory and links them to the exercise of power.

A recent normative theory of discretion couches it in terms of the exercise of practical wisdom (*phronesis*), an Aristotelian idea that brings to bear blended intellectual and moral capacities on public questions. Morgan (1990) argues that public administrators possess *phronesis*, "a special kind of prudence . . . that enables them to coalesce considerations of workability, [popular] acceptability, and fit" with constitutional principles and other key community values. In the American system of government, "it is the deliberative capacity to know how to make the right thing work." Morgan (1990, p. 74) says that this capacity includes the ability to take the broader and longer view and a public interested and constitutionally based understanding of the agency's perspective (pp. 74ff). Morgan and Kass's (1991) research suggests that in actual decision making, the practical wisdom of administrators takes the form of subordinating standards of technical competence and the resolution of competing claims to constitutional principles as administrators interpret them.

To develop a feminist perspective on this notion of practical wisdom, it is necessary to examine the Aristotelian origins of the idea, because Aristotle himself believed women incapable of exercising the form of public judgment that public administration theorists like Morgan now advocate as a model. As we have seen in the examination of other concepts in public administration, feminism is interested in questioning the roots of ideas, to determine whether in the present day they still contain dimensions that work against the interests of women. When we examine what Aristotle had to say about practical wisdom as well as what he had to say about women, we see that a considerable tension exists, one that has ramifications in our own time.

Aristotle's (1976) idea of *phronesis* entails the ability "to deliberate rightly about . . . what is conducive to the good life generally" (Sec. 1140a24); therefore, it blends intellectual and moral capacities. *Phronesis* is acquired through experience at assessing situations in order to determine which elements are relevant to making the right decision, thus it has perceptual as well as rational dimensions. It also involves the emotions; without them, we might miss relevant aspects of situations. *Phronesis* is preeminently a public quality, practiced by those who rule, including citizens.

Aristotle held that women's natural capacities included sexual reproduction and household duties and precluded citizenship. Not only are women suited only for household and child-rearing duties, however, but their realm, though crucial to survival, is inferior to the public world of male citizens (Okin, 1979; Saxonhouse, 1985; Sherman, 1989). Thus admitting women to the company of the practically wise requires a fundamental adjustment in Aristotelian notions of the good society and the good life, which are predicated on a sharp separation between private and public. The root of the problem is that Aristotle's idea of practical wisdom makes it a capacity developed and exercised in public. The essence of citizenship is to interact with fellow citizens in the public space: to listen and speak, to see and be seen, above all to *act* virtuously. In Aristotle's scheme, women are barred from this life. But more serious than that, the viability of men's public life depends on the exclusion of women and slaves: In the balanced and stable society, someone must take the responsibility for managing the necessities of existence if the ultimate good—the leisured political life not bound by the need for results—is to be realized.

But the difficulty goes even deeper, for we are not faced with a vision of society made up of separate but equal spheres, men ruling in public life, women in private. In Aristotle's society, men dominated in *both* spheres. The household is a hierarchy in order that the *polis* need not be. Furthermore, the domination that exists within the household is, by definition, *not political;* therefore, questions about the justice of household arrangements cannot arise. Such practical wisdom as a wife attains is a stunted variety, limited to the lesser concerns of survival.

If practical wisdom requires political practice for its fullest expression and if political practice is only viable given its separation from a realm devoted exclusively to sustenance, then practical wisdom itself depends on this bifurcation between *polis* and household and the subordination of the one to the other. In Aristotle's scheme of things, the household's most notable function is to free men from the exigencies of existence so that they can practice citizenship. The freedom of some, therefore, is purchased at the cost of the unfreedom of others—women and slaves.

In assessing the usefulness of the concept of *phronesis* today, then, when public and private are still (although somewhat less absolutely) divided and when women still bear the primary burden for household affairs, feminists would want to insist that the idea will remain problematic until women are as free as men (in practical terms as well as in theory) to participate in public deliberations, and until men bear an equal responsibility with women for the necessities of life.

The characteristics of *phronesis* are nevertheless interesting from a feminist perspective. Many of the qualities of practical wisdom are strikingly consistent with historically and culturally woman-centered ideas; for example, the rejection of narrow abstracted rationalism in favor of a broader form that encompasses the emotions (a dimension that current theorists of *phronesis* neglect), the stress on the contextuality of practical knowledge and its basis in concrete experience, the acknowledged impossibility of depending solely on rules acquired through formal training and hence the inconsistency with ideas of professional control over events and processes, and the interactive nature of its exercise.

Feminists would want to preserve and promote these qualities in public administrative practice. But they would go further and urge a rendering that severs *phronesis* from dependence on the public-domestic dualism. Feminists would want an understanding of practical wisdom that acknowledges the embodied character of public sector deliberation and action. We need to recognize that most if not all of the concerns of public administration deal with the sustenance and survival of the polity and its individual members. If so, a posture of emotional distance is less appropriate than one that entails engaged objectivity, embodied reason, and the integration of feeling and thought. Harrison (1985) argues that dualistic thinking in moral discourse presents us with apparently irreconcilable alternatives; instead she says, in a suggestion reminiscent of Follett, the essence of justice is a condition under which both my fulfillment and yours become possible. Harrison suggests that at the roots of zero-sum thinking lie patterns of privilege and domination. From her perspective, cutting oneself off from the material conditions of life make one less rather than more qualified for ethical deliberation. Her views expose an inconsistency in Aristotle's idea of *phronesis,* for it would seem that so context-dependent a form of wisdom requires connection rather than distancing from everyday life, including the household, in order to acquire the experience that builds wisdom.

The context in which feminist practical wisdom is grounded includes the influence of gender, race, and class on the life chances of members of the polity; feminist *phronesis* seeks connection with marginalized people in order to ground practice in the real conditions of their lives. Harrison (1985) urges us to resist the temptation to universalize social relations; rather, she says, "moral clarification requires careful attention . . . to the particularity and contingency of human action and social-cultural experience" (p. 65). She reminds us that what is practical in particular about feminist practical wisdom is its roots in and commitment to changing gender/race/class arrangements, which cause real suffering.

A feminist perspective on practical wisdom also requires us to examine its institutional framework. Just as Aristotle envisioned the fullest expression of *phronesis* to entail not simply addressing an individual's personal dilemmas but working out the meaning of the common good in the context of citizenship, so feminist practical wisdom calls on the public administrator to become critically reflective about the agency context within which she or he practices. As a result of women's historical exclusion from the public space, a theme in feminism has been the significance of silences and secrets—of that which is denied, suppressed, excluded. In examining the details of particular agency situations, one must look beyond the overt to that which is usually ignored, not talked about, taken for granted. One must render problematic business as usual, the agency perspective, the accounts people give of their actions. In doing so, however, the practically wise public administrator is likely to encounter dissonance between marginalized needs and perspectives and existing institutional policies and patterns of behavior—a dilemma that may frequently beset with personal risk the decision about what it is right to do given the circumstances.

In administrative discretion guided by feminist practical wisdom, the others one serves, the others one works with, become not abstracted but concrete persons. As Aristotle knew, and as feminism argues, the more knowledge of the particular facets of situations we can uncover and heed, the more rational our ethical reflection becomes.

Thus the feminist charge to public administration is to take seriously an idea of administrative discretion that is concrete, situational, experience-based, interactive, and grounded in perception and feeling as well as in rational analysis. What feminists ask of discretionary judgment in the public sector is to reject public-private, self-other dichotomies. Such conceptual dualisms restrict women's access to the public space and block the transformative power of historically woman-centered ideas. Until we

break free of such imprisoning ways of thinking, public administration will continue to be implicated in gender dynamics that
work material hardships in women's lives and to estrange itself
from the very intellectual and spiritual sources it needs to nourish
a truly practical wisdom.

CONCLUSION

In this concluding chapter, I suggested many of the starting or
entry points through which an analysis of public administration
through the lens of gender might begin to reshape the practice and
the field as we know them. It seems to me that all the answers are
far from obvious at this juncture; besides, for one person to attempt a full-blown vision of public administration transformed by
feminist thinking would strike me as somewhat overweening and,
perhaps more important, a contradiction in terms. This feminist,
at least, is skeptical of visions for their propensity to put people
in their proper places and/or cancel out their own ideas and
dreams. I introduced some different notions into the ongoing
conversation in public administration in the hopes that they will
stimulate people to examine for themselves the gender dilemmas
that lie in terms, concepts, and ideas in good currency.

I do anticipate that if the transformative potential in feminist
ideas were put seriously to work, quite fundamental changes
could occur. One cannot raise questions like the necessity of
hierarchy or the unjust implications of the separation between
public and private without opening up world-shifting vistas. I
would not make the decision about how far we should pursue
these possibilities even if I could. Members of a society must make
such decisions together. But on the other hand, it does not seem
just or sensible to avoid discussing the implications of a gender
analysis of public administration on the basis that it opens up
impossible or threatening prospects.

Ultimately, then, this book serves as an invitation—perhaps a
challenge, too—to others who care about public administration:
Let us not deny the existence of gender dimensions in our images
and ideas, and the dilemmas they pose for women. Let us deal
with them.

References

Adair, D. (1974). *Fame and the founding fathers* (T. Colbourn, Ed.). New York: Norton.

Adams. G. B. (1991, November 1). Personal communication.

Allen, D. G. (1987). Professionalism, occupational segregation by gender, and control of nursing. *Women and Politics, 7,* 1-24.

Allen, J., & Young, I. M. (Eds.). (1989). *The thinking muse: Feminism and modern French philosophy.* Bloomington: Indiana University Press.

Allen, R. L. (1983). *Reluctant reformers: Racism and social reform movements in the United States.* Washington, DC: Howard University Press.

Allen, W. H. (1907). *Efficient democracy.* New York: Dodd, Mead.

Andolsen, B. H. (1986). *"Daughters of Jefferson, daughters of bootblacks": Racism and American feminism.* Macon, GA: Mercer University Press.

Argyris, C. (1957). *Personality and organization.* New York: Harper.

Aristotle. (1976). *The Nichomachean ethics* (J. A. K. Thomson, Trans.). Harmondsworth, UK: Penguin.

Aristotle. (1981). *The politics* (T. A. Sinclair, Trans.). Harmondsworth, UK: Penguin.

Aron, C. S. (1987). *Ladies and gentlemen of the civil service: Middle class workers in Victorian America.* New York: Oxford University Press.

Astin, H. S., & Leland, C. (1991). *Women of influence, women of vision: A cross-generational study of leaders and social change.* San Francisco: Jossey-Bass.

Baker, P. (1990). The domestication of politics: Women and American political society, 1780-1920. In L. Gordon (Ed.), *Women, the state, and welfare* (pp. 55-91). Madison: University of Wisconsin.

Baker, R. S. (1968). *Woodrow Wilson: Life and letters. Vol. 4: President, 1913-1914.* New York: Greenwood. (Original work published 1931)

Barnard, C. I. (1938). *The functions of the executive.* Cambridge, MA: Harvard University Press.

Barnard, C. I. (1948). *Organization and management: Selected papers.* Cambridge: Harvard University Press.

Beard, M. (1972). *Women's work in municipalities.* New York: Arno. (Original work published 1915)

Bell, D. (1987). *And we are not saved: The elusive quest for racial justice.* New York: Basic Books.

Bellavita, C. (1986, Fall). The organization of leadership. *The Bureaucrat,* pp. 13-16.

Bellavita, C. (1991). The public administrator as hero. *Administration and Society, 23*(2), 155-185.

Bennis, W. G., & Nanus, B. (1985). *Leaders: The strategies for taking charge.* New York: Harper & Row.

Blagdon, H. W. (1967). *Woodrow Wilson: The academic years.* Cambridge, MA: Belknap Press.

Bledstein, B. J. (1976). *The culture of professionalism: The middle class and the development of higher education in America.* New York: Norton.

Bloch, R. H. (1987). The gendered meanings of virtue in revolutionary America. *Signs: Journal of Women in Culture and Society, 13*(1), 37-58.

Blum, L. A. (1988). Moral exemplars: Reflections on Schindler, the Trocmes, and others. *Midwest Studies in Philosophy, 12,* 196-221.

Bologh, R. W. (1990). *Love or greatness: Max Weber and masculine thinking—a feminist inquiry.* London: Unwin Hyman.

Bordo, S. (1987). The Cartesian masculinization of thought. In S. Harding & J. F. O'Barr (Eds.), *Sex and scientific inquiry* (pp. 247-264). Chicago: University of Chicago.

Braudy, L. (1986). *The frenzy of renown: Fame and its history.* New York: Oxford University Press.

Brooks-Higgenbotham, E. (1989). The problem of race in women's history. In E. Weed (Ed.), *Coming to terms: Feminism, theory, politics* (pp. 122-133). New York: Routledge.

Brown, W. (1988). *Manhood and politics: A feminist reading in political theory.* Totowa, NJ: Rowman & Littlefield.

Bruere, H. (1981). Efficiency in city government. In F. C. Mosher (Ed.), *Basic literature of American public administration, 1787-1950* (pp. 92-95). New York: Holmes & Meier. (Original work published 1912)

Butler, M. (1978). Early liberal roots of feminism: John Locke and the attack on patriarchy. *American Political Science Review, 72,* 135-150.

Caldwell, L. K. (1988). *The Administrative theories of Hamilton and Jefferson: Their contribution to thought on public administration* (2nd ed.). New York: Holmes & Meier.

Carby, H. V. (1986). On the threshold of woman's era: Lynching, empire, and sexuality in black feminist theory. In H. L. Gates, Jr. (Ed.), *"Race," writing and difference* (pp. 301-316). Chicago: University of Chicago Press.

Chodorow, N. (1978). *The reproduction of mothering: Psychoanalysis and the sociology of gender.* Berkeley: University of California Press.

Cigler, B. A. (1990). Public administration and the paradox of professionalization. *Public Administration Review, 50*(6), 637-653.

Clark, L. M. G. (1979). Women and Locke: Who owns the apple in the garden of Eden? In L. M. G. Clark & L. Lange (Eds.), *The sexism of social and political theory: Women and reproduction from Plato to Nietzsche* (pp. 16-40). Toronto: University of Toronto Press.

Clinton, C. (1984). *The other civil war: American women in the nineteenth century.* New York: Hill & Wang.

Cocks, J. (1989). *The oppositional imagination: Feminism, critique and political theory.* London: Routledge.

Cooke, J. E. (Ed.). (1961). *The federalist.* Middletown, CT: Wesleyan University Press.

Cooper, T. L. (1984a). Citizenship and professionalism in public administration [Special issue] (H. G. Frederickson & R. C. Chandler, Eds.). *Public Administration Review, 44,* 143-149.

Cooper, T. L. (1984b). Public administration in an age of scarcity: A citizenship role for public administrators. In J. Rabin & J. S. Bowman (Eds.), *Politics and administration: Woodrow Wilson and American public administration* (pp. 297-314). New York: Marcel Dekker.

Cooper, T. L. (1991). *An ethic of citizenship for public administration.* Englewood Cliffs, NJ: Prentice-Hall.

Cooper, T. L., & Wright, N. D. (Eds.). (1992). *Exemplary public administrators: Character and leadership in government.* San Franciso: Jossey-Bass.

Cott, N. F. (1977). *The bonds of womanhood: "Women's sphere" in New England, 1780-1830.* New Haven, CT: Yale University Press.

Crenson, M. A. (1975). *The federal machine: Beginnings of bureaucracy in Jacksonian America.* Baltimore: Johns Hopkins University Press.

Croly, H. (1963). *The promise of American life.* New York: E. P. Dutton. (Original work published 1909)

De Beauvoir, S. (1961). *The second sex* (H. M. Parshley, Trans.). New York: Bantam.

Denhardt, R. B., & Perkins, J. (1976). The coming death of administrative man. *Public Administration Review, 36*(4), 379-384.

Derber, C. (1983). Managing professionals: Ideological proletarianization and post-industrial labor. *Theory and Society, 12,* 309-341.

Doig, J. W. (1988, September). *Leadership and innovation in the administrative state.* Paper presented at the Minnowbrook II meeting, Minnowbrook, NY.

Doig, J. W., & Hargrove, E. C. (Eds.). (1987). *Leadership and innovation: A biographical perspective on entrepreneurs in government.* Baltimore: Johns Hopkins University Press.

Edwards, L. R. (1984). *Psyche as hero: Female heroism and fictional form.* Middletown, CT: Wesleyan University Press.

Epstein, C. F. (1988). *Deceptive distinctions: Sex, gender and the social order.* New Haven, CT: Yale University Press.

Etzoni, A. (1969). *The semi-professions and their organizations.* New York: Free Press.

Faludi, S. (1991). *Backlash: The undeclared war against American women.* New York: Crown.

Ferguson, K. E. (1984). *The feminist case against bureaucracy.* Philadelphia: Temple University Press.

"Few women found in top public jobs." (1992, January 3). *New York Times,* p. A8.

Fierman, J. (1990, July). Why women still don't hit the top. *Fortune,* pp. 30, 40-42, 50, 54, 58, 62.

Finer, H. (1984). Administrative responsibility in a democratic government. In F. E. Rourke (Ed.), *Bureaucratic power in national government* (3rd ed., pp. 410-421). Boston: Little, Brown. (Original work published in 1941)

Finley, M. I. (1965). *The world of Odysseus* (rev. ed.). New York: Viking.

Fisher, B. (1988). Wandering in the wilderness: The search for women role models. *Signs: Journal of Women in Culture and Society, 13*(2), 211-233.

Fitzpatrick, E. (1990). *Endless crusade: Women social scientists and Progressive reform.* New York: Oxford University Press.

Fox, C., & Cochran, C. E. (1990). Discretionary public administration: Toward a platonic guardian class. In H. Kass and B. Catron (Eds.), *Images and identities in public administration* (pp. 87-112). Newbury Park, CA: Sage.

Follett, M. P. (1951). *Creative experience.* Gloucester, MA: Peter Smith. (Original work published 1924)

Follett, M. P. (1965). *The new state.* New York: Peter Smith. (Original work published 1918)

Franzway, S., Court, D., & Connell, R. W. (1989). *Staking a claim: Feminism, bureaucracy and the state.* Sydney: Allen & Unwin.

Fraser, N. (1990). Talking about needs: Interpretive contests as political conflicts. In C. R. Sunstein (Ed.), *Feminism and political theory* (pp. 159-181). Chicago: University of Chicago Press.

Frederickson, H. G., & Hart, D. K. (1985). The public service and the patriotism of benevolence. *Public Administration Review, 45*(5), 547-554.

Friedrich, C. J. (1984). Public policy and the nature of administrative responsibility. In F. E. Rourke (Ed.), *Bureaucratic power in national politics* (3rd ed., pp. 399-409). Boston: Little, Brown. (Original work published in 1940)

Gallas, N. M. (1976). Introductory comments. In N. M. Gallas (Ed.), A symposium: Women in public administration. *Public Administration Review, 36*(4), 347-349.

Gawthrop, L. A. (1984). Civis, civitas, and civilitas: A new focus for the year 2000 [Special issue] (H. G. Frederickson & R. C. Chandler, Eds.). *Public Administration Review, 44,* 101-107.

Gawthrop, L. A. (1987). Toward an ethical convergence of democratic theory and administrative politics. In R. C. Chandler (Ed.), *A centennial history of the American administrative state* (pp. 189-216). New York: Free Press.

Ginzberg, L. D. (1990). *Women and the work of benevolence: Morality, politics, and class in the 19th century United States.* New Haven, CT: Yale University Press.

Giddings, P. (1985). *When and where I enter: The impact of black women on race and sex in America.* New York: Bantam.

Gilligan, C. (1982). *In a different voice: Psychological theory and women's development.* Cambridge, MA: Harvard University Press.

Glazer, P. M., & Slater, M. (1987). *Unequal colleagues: The entrance of women into the professions, 1890-1940.* New Brunswick, NJ: Rutgers University Press.

Goodnow, F. J. (1981). Politics and administration. In F. C. Mosher (Ed.), *Basic literature of American public administration, 1787-1950* (pp. 82-92). New York: Holmes & Meier. (Original work published 1900)

Goodsell, C. T. (1985). *The case for bureaucracy* (2nd ed.). Chatham NJ: Chatham House.

Gordon, L. (Ed.). (1990). *Women, the state, and welfare.* Madison: University of Wisconsin Press.

Green, R. T. (1988). The Hamiltonian image of the public administrator: Public administrators as prudent constitutionalists. *Dialogue: The Public Administration Theory Network, 10*(3), 25-53.

Grenier, G. (1988). *Inhuman relations: Quality circles and anti-unionism in American industry.* Philadelphia: Temple University Press.

Grosz, E. (1990). *Jacques Lacan: A feminist introduction.* London: Routledge.

Grubb, B. (1991, Winter). The quiet revolution of Bev Forbes. *Seattle University News,* pp. 18-19.

Gutek, B. A. (1989). Sexuality in the workplace: Key issues in social research and organizational practice. In J. Hearn, D. L. Sheppard, P. Tancred-Sheriff, & G. Burrell (Eds.), *The Sexuality of Organization* (pp. 56-70). London: Sage.

Haber, S. (1964). *Efficiency and uplift: Scientific management in the Progressive era 1890-1920.* Chicago: University of Chicago Press.

Habermas, J. (1972). *Knowledge and human interests.* London: Heinemann.

Hale, M. M., & Kelly, R. M. (Eds.). (1989). *Gender, bureaucracy, and democracy: Careers and equal opportunity in the public sector.* Westport, CT: Greenwood Press.

Harding, S. (1986). *The science question in feminism.* Ithaca, NY: Cornell University Press.

Harley, S. (1990). For the good of family and race: Gender, work and domestic roles in the black community, 1880-1930. In M. R. Malson, E. Mudimbe-Boyi, J. F. O'Barr, & M. Wyer (Eds.), *Black Women in America: Social Science Perspectives* (pp. 159-172). Chicago: University of Chicago Press.

Harragan, B. (1981). *Games mother never taught you.* New York: Warner.

Harrison, B. W. (1985). *Making the connections: Essays in feminist social ethics* (C. S. Robb, Ed.). Boston: Beacon Press.

Hearn, J., & Parkin, P. W. (1988). Women, men, and leadership: A critical review of assumptions, practice and change in the industrialized nations. In N. J. Adler & D. N. Israeli (Eds.), *Women in management worldwide* (pp. 17-40). Armonk, NY: Sharpe.

Helgesen, S. (1990). *The female advantage: Women's ways of leadership.* New York: Doubleday.

Heller, T. (1982). *Women and men as leaders: In business, educational and social service organizations.* New York: Praeger.

Hochschild, A. (1989). *The second shift: Working parents and the revolution at home.* New York: Viking.

Holusha, J. (1991, May 5). Grace Pastiak's "web of inclusion." *New York Times,* sec. 3, pp. 1, 6.

Hudson Institute. (1988). *Civil service 2000.* Washington DC: U.S. Government Printing Office.

" 'Iron Lady' attacks sexual political double standard." (1990, September 14). *The Olympian,* p. A1.

Jaggar, A. (1983). *Feminist politics and human nature.* Totowa, NJ: Rowman & Allenheld.

Johnson, B. (1987). *A world of difference.* Baltimore: Johns Hopkins University Press.

Johnson, T. H. (1960). *The complete poems of Emily Dickinson.* Boston: Little, Brown.

Kanter, R. M. (1977). *Men and women of the corporation.* New York: Basic Books.

Kanter, R. M. (1980). Women and the structure of organizations: Explorations in theory and behavior. In C. W. Konek, S. L. Kitch, & G. E. Hammond (Eds.), *Design for equity: Women and leadership in higher education* (pp. 49-63). Newton, MA: Educational Development Center.

Kass, H. D. (1990). Stewardship as a fundamental element in images of public administration. In H. D. Kass & B. L. Catron (Eds.), *Images and identities in public administration* (pp. 113-131). Newbury Park, CA: Sage.

Kass, H. D., & Catron, B. L. (Eds.). (1990). *Images and identities in public administration.* Newbury Park, CA: Sage.

Kearny, R. C., & Sinha, C. (1988). Professionalism and bureaucratic responsiveness: Conflict or compatibility. *Public Administration Review, 48*(1), 571-579.

Keller, E. F. (1985). *Reflections on gender and science.* New Haven, CT: Yale University Press.

Keller, E. F., & Grontkowski, C. (1983). The mind's eye. In S. Harding & M. B. Hintikka (Eds.), *Discovering Reality* (pp. 207-224). Dordrecht, The Netherlands: Reidel.

Keller, L. F. (1988). A heritage from Rome: The administrator as doer. *Dialogue: The Public Administration Theory Network, 10*(2), 49-75.

Kelley, R. E. (1989). In praise of followers. In W. E. Rosenbach & R. L. Taylor (Eds.), *Contemporary issues in leadership* (2nd ed., pp. 124-134). Boulder, CO: Westview Press.

Kelly, R. M. (1991). *The gendered economy.* Newbury Park, CA: Sage.

Kerber, L. K. (1980). *Women of the republic: Intellect and ideology in revolutionary America.* New York: Norton.

Kets de Vries, M. F. R. (1989). *Prisons of leadership.* New York: John Wiley.

King, C. S. (1992). *Gender and management: Men, women and decision-making in public organizations.* Unpublished doctoral dissertation, University of Colorado, Denver.

Kotter, J. P. (1990, May-June). What leaders really do. *Harvard Business Review,* pp. 103-111.

Kraditor, A. (1968). *Up from the pedestal: Selected writing in the history of American feminism.* Chicago: Quadrangle Books.

Krislov, S. (1974). *Representative bureaucracy.* Englewood Cliffs, NJ: Prentice-Hall.

Kruse, L., & Wintermantel, M. (1986). Leadership ms-qualified I: The gender bias in everyday and scientific thinking. In C. F. Graumann & S. Moscovici (Eds.), *Changing conceptions of leadership* (pp. 171-198). New York: Springer-Verlag.

Kuhn, T. S. (1970). *The structure of scientific revolutions* (2nd ed.). Chicago: University of Chicago Press.

Landes, J. B. (1988). *Women and the public sphere in the age of the French revolution.* Ithaca, NY: Cornell University Press.

Lane, L. M., & Wolf, J. F. (1990). *The human resources crisis in the public sector: Rebuilding the capacity to govern.* Westport, CT: Quorum Books.

Lange, L. (1979). Rousseau and the general will. In L. M. G. Clark & L. Lang (Eds.), *The sexism of social and political theory: Women and reproduction from Plato to Nietzsche* (pp. 41-52). Toronto: University of Toronto Press.

Lawlor, J. (1991, August 9). Labor Department shrugs off 'glass ceiling' study. *USA Today*, p. 1B.

Laws, J. L. (1976). Work aspirations of women: False leads and new starts. In M. Blaxall & B. Reagan (Eds.), *Women and the workplace: The implications of occupational segregation* (pp. 33-50). Chicago: University of Chicago Press.

Leach, W. (1980). *True love and perfect union: The feminist reform of sex and society.* New York: Basic Books.

LeGuin, U. (1974). *The left hand of darkness.* Ace Books.

Lemons, J. S. (1990). *The woman citizen: Social feminism in the 1920s.* Charlottesville: University of Virginia Press. (Original work published 1973)

Lerner, G. (1979). *The majority finds its past: Placing women in history.* New York: Oxford University Press.

Lerner, G. (1986). *The creation of patriarchy.* New York: Oxford University Press.

Lewis, E. (1980). *Public entrepreneurship: Toward a theory of bureaucratic political power.* Bloomington: Indiana University Press.

Long, N. E. (1981). The S.E.S. and the public interest. *Public Administration Review, 41*(3), 305-311.

Lubove, R. (1965). *Professional altruism: The emergence of social work as a career 1880-1930.* Cambridge, MA: Harvard University Press.

Lugones, M. (1991). On the logic of pluralist feminism. In C. Card (Ed.), *Feminist ethics* (pp. 35-44). Lawrence: University of Kansas Press.

Maccoby, M. (1988). *Why work: Motivating and leading the new generation.* New York: Simon & Schuster.

Mainzer, L. C. (1964, January). Honor in bureaucratic life. *Review of Politics, 26,* 70-90.

Manning, M. (1989). *Leadership skills for women: Achieving impact as a manager* (with P. Haddock). Los Altos, CA: Crisp.

Markus, M. (1987). Women, success and civil society: Submission to, or subversion of, the achievement principle. In S. Benhabib & D. Cornell (Eds.), *Feminism as critique* (pp. 96-109). Minneapolis: University of Minnesota Press.

Merchant, C. (1980). *The death of nature: Women, ecology, and the scientific revolution.* San Francisco: Harper & Row.

Milwid, B. (1990). *Working with men: Professional women talk about power, sexuality, and ethics.* Hillsboro, OR: Beyond Words Publishing.

Mintzberg, H. (1973). *The nature of managerial work.* New York: Harper & Row.

Mitchell, T. (1991). The limits of the state: Beyond statist approaches and their critics. *American Political Science Review, 85*(1), 79-96.

Mitchell, T. R., & Scott, W. G. (1987). Leadership failures, the distrusting public, and prospects of the administrative state. *Public Administration Review, 47*(6), 445-452.

Moi, T. (1985). *Sexual/textual politics: Feminist literary theory.* London: Routledge.

Moore, H. (1988). *Feminism and anthropology.* Minneapolis: University of Minnesota Press.

Morgan, D. F. (1990). Administrative *phronesis*: Discretion and the problem of administrative legitimacy in our constitutional system. In H. D. Kass & B. L. Catron (Eds.), *Images and identities in public administration* (pp. 67-86). Newbury Park, CA: Sage.

Morgan, D. F., & Kass, H. D. (1991). Constitutional stewardship, *phronesis* and the American administrative ethos. *Dialogue: The Public Administration Theory Network, 12*(1), 17-60.

Mosher, F. C. (1968). *Democracy and the Public Service.* New York: Oxford University Press.

Nalbandian, J. (1990). Tenets of contemporary professionalism in local government. *Public Administration Review, 50*(6), 654-662.

Neverdon-Morton, C. (1989). *Afro-American women of the South and the advancement of the race, 1895-1925.* Knoxville: University of Tennessee Press.

O'Brien, M. (1989). *Reproducing the world: Essays in feminist theory.* Boulder, CO: Westview.

O'Leary, R., & Wise, C. R. (1991). Public managers, judges, and legislators: Redefining the new partnership. *Public Administration Review, 51*(4), 316-327.

Okin, S. M. (1979). *Women in Western political thought.* Princeton, NJ: Princeton University Press.

Okin, S. M. (1989). *Justice, gender and the family.* New York: Basic Books.

Perry, J. L. (1989). *Handbook of public administration.* San Francisco: Jossey-Bass.

Peterson, I. (1992, February 2). These data, the enumerator always wrings twice. *New York Times,* p. E3.

Pitkin, H. F. (1984). *Fortune is a woman: Gender and politics in the thought of Niccolo Machiavelli.* Berkeley: University of California Press.

Poggi, G. (1978). *The development of the modern state: A sociological introduction.* Stanford, CA: Stanford University Press.

Poggi, G. (1990). *The state: Its nature, development and prospects.* Stanford, CA: Stanford University Press.

Potts, M., & Behr, P. (1987). *The leading edge: CEOs who turned their companies around: What they did and how they did it.* New York: McGraw-Hill.

Powell, G. N. (1988). *Women and men in management.* Newbury Park, CA: Sage.

Pringle, R. (1989). Bureaucracy, rationality, and sexuality: The case of secretaries. In J. Hearn, D. L. Sheppard, P. Tancred-Sheriff, & G. Burrell (Eds.), *The sexuality of organization* (pp. 158-177). London: Sage.

Pugh, D. L. (1989). Professionalism in public administration: Problems, perspectives and the role of ASPA. *Public Administration Review, 49*(1), 1-8.

Rhode, D. (1988). Perspectives on professional women. *Stanford Law Review, 40,* 1163-1207.

Rohr, J. A. (1986). *To run a constitution: The legitimacy of the American administrative state.* Lawrence: University of Kansas Press.

Rohr, J. A. (1989). Public administration, executive power and constitutional confusion. *Public Administration Review, 49*(2), 108-114.

Rosenbloom, D. H. (1987). Public administrators and the judiciary: The 'new partnership.' *Public Administration Review, 47*(1), 75-83.

Rosener, J. B. (1990, November-December). Ways women lead. *Harvard Business Review*, pp. 119-125.

Rossi, A. S. (Ed.). (1973). *The feminist papers: From Adams to De Beauvoir*. New York: Columbia University Press.

Ruddick, S. (1989). *Maternal thinking: Toward a politics of peace*. Boston: Beacon.

Saltzman, A. (1991, June 17). Trouble at the top. *U.S. News and World Report*. pp. 40-48.

Saxonhouse, A. (1985). *Women in the history of political thought*. New York: Praeger.

Scott, J. W. (1989). Gender: A useful category of historical analysis. In E. Weed (Ed.), *Coming to terms: Feminism, theory, politics* (pp. 81-100). New York: Routledge.

Selznick, P. (1957). *Leadership in administration: A sociological interpretation*. Evanston, IL: Row, Peterson.

Sheppard, D. L. (1989). Organizations, power and sexuality: The image and self-image of women managers. In J. Hearn, D. L. Sheppard, P. Tancred-Sheriff, & G. Burrell (Eds.), *The Sexuality of organization* (pp. 139-157). London: Sage.

Sherman, N. (1989). *The fabric of character: Aristotle's theory of virtue*. Oxford, UK: Clarendon Press.

Skowronek, S. (1982). *Building a new American state: The expansion of national administrative capacities 1877-1920*. Cambridge, UK: Cambridge University Press.

Smircich, L. (1985). *Toward a woman-centered organization theory*. Paper presented at the symposium on women and social change, Academy of Management, San Diego, CA.

Sterling, D. (Ed.). (1984). *We are your sisters: Black women in the nineteenth century*. New York: Norton.

Stever, J. A. (1988). *The end of public administration: Problems of the profession in the post-Progressive era*. Dobbs Ferry, NY: Transnational.

Stewart, D. W. (1976). Women in top jobs: An opportunity for federal leadership. *Public Administration Review, 36*(4), 357-364.

Stillman, R. J. (1991). *Preface to public administration: A search for themes and direction*. New York: St. Martins.

Stivers, C. (1990a). Active citizenship and public administration. In G. Wamsley, R. Bacher, C. Goodsell, P. Kronenberg, J. Rohr, C. Stivers, O. White, & J. Wolf, *Refounding Public Administration* (pp. 246-273). Newbury Park, CA: Sage.

Stivers, C. (1990b). Toward a feminist theory of public administration. *Women and Politics, 10*(4), 49-65.

Stivers, C. (1991). Why can't a woman be less like a man? Women's leadership dilemma. *Journal of Nursing Administration, 21*(5), 47-51.

Stivers, C. (1992a). Beverlee A. Myers: Power, virtue and womanhood in public administration. In T. L. Cooper and N. D. Wright (Eds.), *Exemplary public administrators: Character and leadership in government* (pp. 166-192). San Francisco: Jossey-Bass.

Stivers, C. (1992b). "A wild patience": A feminist critique of ameliorative public administration. In M. T. Bailey & R. T. Mayer (Eds.), *Public management in an interconnected world: Essays in the Minnowbrook tradition* (pp. 53-74). Westport, CT: Greenwood.

Taylor, F. W. (1911). *The principles of scientific management*. New York: Harper & Brothers.

Terry, L. D. (1990). Leadership in the administrative state: The concept of administrative conservatorship. *Administration and Society, 21*(4), 395-412.

Terry, L. D. (1991). The public administrator as hero: All that glitters is not gold: Rejoinder to Christopher Bellavita's "The private administrator as hero." *Administration and Society, 23*(1), 186-193.

Thompson, K. W. (1985). *The credibility of institutions, policies and leadership. Vol. 18: Essays on leadership: Comparative insights.* Lanham, MD: University Press of America.

Tichy, N., & Ulrich, D. (1984). Revitalizing organizations: The leadership role. In J. R. Kimberley & R. E. Quinn (Eds.), *New futures: The challenge of managing corporate transitions* (pp. 240-265). Homewood, IL: Dow Jones Irwin.

Travis, D. J. (1991). *Racism American style: A corporate gift.* Chicago: Urban Research Press.

U.S. Bureau of the Census. (1940). *Statistical abstract of the United States.* Washington, DC: U.S. Government Printing Office.

U.S. Bureau of the Census. (1960). *Statistical abstract of the United States.* Washington, DC: U.S. Government Printing Office.

U.S. Bureau of the Census. (1990). *Statistical abstract of the United States.* Washington, DC: U.S. Government Printing Office.

Van Riper, P. P. (1983). The American administrative state: Wilson and the founders—An unorthodox view. *Public Administration Review, 43*(6), 477-490.

Vollmer, H. M., & Mills, D. L. (Eds.). (1966). *Professionalization.* Englewood Cliffs, NJ: Prentice-Hall.

Waldo, D. (1948). *The administrative state.* New York: Ronald Press.

Wamsley, G. L. (1990). The agency perspective: Public administrators as agential leaders. In G. L. Wamsley, R. N. Bacher, C. T. Goodsell, P. S. Kronenberg, J. A. Rohr, C. M. Stivers, O. F. White, & J. F. Wolf, *Refounding public administration* (pp. 114-162). Newbury Park, CA: Sage.

Wamsley, G. L., Bacher, R. N., Goodsell, C. T., Kronenberg, P. S., Rohr, J. A., Stivers, C. M., White, O. F., & Wolf, J. F. (1990). *Refounding public administration.* Newbury Park, CA: Sage.

Warner, M. (1981). *Joan of Arc: The image of female heroism.* New York: Knopf.

Wells, T. (1973, Summer). The covert power of gender in organizations. *Journal of Contemporary Business,* pp. 53-68.

Welter, B. (1976). The cult of true womanhood 1820-1860. In B. Welter, *Dimity convictions: The American woman in the 19th century* (pp. 21-41). Athens: Ohio University Press.

White, L. D. (1948). *The federalists.* New York: Macmillan.

White, L. D. (1951). *The Jeffersonians.* New York: Macmillan.

Wiebe, R. H. (1967). *The search for order 1877-1920.* New York: Hill & Wang.

Wildavsky, A. (1990). Administration without hierarchy? Bureaucracy without authority? In N. B. Lynn & A. Wildavsky (Eds.), *Public administration: The state of the discipline* (pp. xiii-xix). Chatham, NJ: Chatham House.

Wills, G. (1984). *Cincinnatus: George Washington and the enlightenment.* Garden City, NY: Doubleday.

Wilson, J. Q. (1989). *Bureaucracy: What government agencies do and why they do it.* New York: Basic.

Wilson, W. (1978). The study of administration. In J. M. Shafritz & A. C. Hyde (Eds.), *Classics of public administration* (pp. 3-17). Oak Park, IL: Moore. (Original work published 1887)

Wyzomirski, M. J. (1987). The politics of art: Nancy Hanks and the National Endowment for the Arts. In J. W. Doig & E. C. Hargrove (Eds.), *Leadership and innovation: A biographical perspective on entrepreneurs in government* (pp. 207-245). Baltimore: Johns Hopkins University Press.

Young, I. M. (1987). Impartiality and the civic public. In S. Benhabib & D. Cornell (Eds.), *Feminism as critique* (pp. 57-76). Minneapolis, University of Minnesota Press.

Index

157

About the Author

Camilla Stivers received a B.A. degree from Wellesley College, an M.P.A. degree from the University of Southern California, and a Ph.D. in Public Administration and Policy from Virginia Polytechnic Institute and State University. She had a 20-year career as an administrator in public and nonprofit organizations, specializing in health care and community development. In 1986-1987, she was Associate Study Director for the National Academy of Sciences/Institute of Medicine report, *The Future of Public Health.* Since 1987, she has taught public administration at The Evergreen State College, Olympia, Washington. She is a co-author of the book *Refounding Public Administration,* and her work has appeared in several collections and scholarly journals. She is a member of the editorial board of *Administration and Society* and the advisory board of *Signs: Journal of Women in Culture and Society*. She has served on the National Council of the American Society for Public Administration.